How Organizations Learn

Anthony J. DiBella
Edwin C. Nevis

How Organizations Learn

An Integrated Strategy for Building Learning Capability

Jossey-Bass Publishers
San Francisco

Substantial discounts on bulk quantities of Jossey-Bass books are available to corporations, professional associations, and other organizations. For details and discount information, contact the special sales department at Jossey-Bass Inc., Publishers (415) 433–1740; Fax (800) 605–2665.

For sales outside the United States, please contact your local Simon & Schuster International Office.

Jossey-Bass Web address: http://www.josseybass.com

 Manufactured in the United States of America on Lyons Falls Turin Book. This paper is acid-free and 100 percent totally chlorine-free.

Library of Congress Cataloging-in-Publication Data

DiBella, Anthony J., 1948–
   How organizations learn : an integrated strategy for building
    learning capability / Anthony J. DiBella, Edwin C. Nevis. — 1st ed.
      p. cm. — (The Jossey-Bass business & management series)
    Includes bibliographical references and index.
    ISBN 0–7879–1107–0 (acid-free paper)
   1. Organizational learning. I. Nevis, Edwin C. II. Title.
   III. Series.
   HD58.82.D53 1998
   658.4'06—dc21
                                97–21112
                                  CIP

FIRST EDITION
HB Printing 10 9 8 7 6 5 4 3 2 1

The Jossey-Bass
Business & Management Series

For my children—
Ana Lucia and Samuel Anthony
A.J.D.

And for my grandchildren—
Aaron and Samuel
E.C.N.

Contents

Part III: Adapting and Assessing the Learning Strategy

Preface

The aim of this book is to help readers understand and increase the capability of their organizations to learn. Unless businesses develop their capability to learn, they are apt to suffer from such disabling tendencies as marketing myopia, groupthink, the not-invented-here syndrome, and "reinventing the wheel." For example, had the American nuclear power industry not learned from the 1976 accident at Three Mile Island, there would be no nuclear power industry today. On the other hand, had that industry focused on learning capability prior to 1976, Three Mile Island might not have occurred and the industry could be growing today instead of declining.

It is our intention to make sense, for practitioners and academicians, of the burgeoning literature on organizational learning and to present a set of ideas that are useful to extend both research and business performance. A major contribution is to build on various approaches to organizational learning to create a new foundation for what organizations must do to develop learning capability. How do our companies and organizations process their experiences to learn from them and how can they handle this responsibility better? We do not want to simply point out what needs to be done. We also want this book to address the issue of implementation—that is, how learning capability can be developed through changes in attitudes, behaviors, and structures.

Our approach to organizational learning is based on extensive knowledge of the literature about organizational learning, what learning organizations are, and how they can be created; in-depth research in seven American and European companies that focused on understanding how and why organizations learn; and field experience with more than twenty-five Fortune 500 companies in testing and using materials we have developed in collaboration with executive managers, human resource and organization development consultants and trainers, and operations staff to build learning capability. Readers of this book will acquire an in-depth understanding of concepts related to organizational learning and the "learning organization" as well as a set of practical techniques.

During the past five years interest in organizational learning has grown at a seemingly exponential rate, especially following the publication of Peter Senge's book *The Fifth Discipline* (1990). The roots of current practitioner and scholarly interest in organizational learning go back to the total quality movement of the 1970s and 1980s and its focus on continuous improvement or incremental learning, and before that to the notion that organizations comprise systems of decision making (March and Simon, 1958), knowledge acquisition (Cyert and March, 1963), and core competence (Prahalad and Hamel, 1990). Scholars and practitioners have based their prescriptions on specific assumptions about learning and about organizations. Sets of assumptions form frameworks or perspectives of understanding and platforms for action. For example, some authors have focused on the unique attributes or required characteristics of organizational learning (normative perspective); some have focused on the need for organizations to develop through a series of distinct stages (developmental perspective); and some have recognized the learning properties in and of all organizations (capabilities perspective). Although each perspective adds to our understanding of organizational learning, each alone provides a limited or fragmented view of how learning capability can be developed. We call our approach "integrated" because it combines elements from each perspective. The result is a more comprehensive, realistic, and productive framework for building learning capability in organizations.

Organizational learning has great potential for improving performance or business outcomes, but it can be an intimidating or confusing pursuit. Though there is an abundance of concepts, some are poorly defined or simply provide no consensus on what organizational learning is or why it occurs. For example, can we assume that something taught means something learned? Must learning manifest itself as behavior? If the employees of a company learn a new skill, can we say that the company or organization has learned too?

When we fly in an airplane in the United States, the Federal Aviation Administration (FAA) requires that passengers be instructed how to put on a life vest. Yet in the confines of an airplane, we never actually put on our life vests unless our lives are clearly in danger, when learning how to means learning too late. The FAA just presumes that we have learned. The example brings up another complication about learning: separating the process from the content. What good does it do if an airplane passenger has learned to put on a life vest backward? Learning may have occurred, but what has been learned may not lead to optimal results. Until recently, for instance, ValuJet Airlines had learned how to run an airline cheaply but not well, with tragic consequences.

These examples illustrate a few dilemmas about learning in general but raise questions about comparing the learning of individuals with the learning of organizations. Airplanes do not learn how to put on life vests, humans do—or at least they are instructed how to. Yet organizational learning is real. Without seventy-five years or so of organizational learning about how to design, build, operate, and maintain aircraft, no one today would be flying to Europe or elsewhere. While humans have been learning how to put life vests on, Boeing Corporation has been learning how to design and build safer aircraft; General Electric, Pratt & Whitney, and Rolls-Royce have been learning how to design and build more efficient and more reliable aircraft engines; and airline companies have been learning how best to maintain their planes. Some of this learning occurred because the National Transportation Safety Board studied civilian aircraft accidents to learn how they could be avoided in the future.

Organizational learning has been a critical process for ensuring the very existence of whole industries. Aerospace, nuclear power, and agrochemical processing are industries in addition to civilian aviation whose very survival is dependent on learning from experience. Entirely new products and industries would not have been spawned without organizational learning: home computers, cellular phones, central air conditioning, power tools. Many start-up companies are the result of learning that cannot be implemented in established companies. The idea, product, or technology that spawns a start-up is often contrary or countercultural to an established firm's core competence.

What, how, and how well an organization learns has everything to do with its ability to compete. Given how critical continual improvement is in today's marketplace, it is nearly impossible to avoid the declarations that companies need to learn faster and faster just to stay in the same place. However, learning does not just happen; it is more often the result of deliberate effort that takes time and resources. When companies are faced with so many economic and competitive pressures, why learn? That is, why should companies take organizational learning seriously and make it a strategic priority? The question is exceedingly simple to state but fundamental and sometimes difficult for managers to answer as they choose methods to enhance the effectiveness of their firms, business units, and work teams. It takes time to see the benefits of learning; so many managers are seduced by the "quick fix" of other interventions, such as downsizing, that can improve the bottom line on the next quarterly report. The problem, as most of us realize, is that there are hidden, long-term costs to interventions that focus on short-term results. Reductions in force and early retirement programs may reduce today's labor costs but may also have the unintended outcome of lost organizational learning: as experienced workers leave, they carry out the door a source of knowledge that gave the firm its competitive advantage.

The hidden value of learning is best expressed in this adage: "If you think education is expensive, try ignorance." Businesses and organizations operating in today's postindustrial era are confronted by ongoing change in just about every domain that affects their performance, including technology, demographics, and consumer preferences. To survive, their most critical core competence is not what makes them successful today but their ability to learn about and adapt to change so they can compete tomorrow. Firms also face the challenges of increasing globalization and competitiveness. These forces require firms to continually improve their operations by learning from their own experience or from benchmarking against others.

To build learning capability, managers and practitioners need to take advantage of what the literature is saying and how it applies to their organizations. This book presents a framework that builds on the best of established theory and is both diagnostic and prescriptive. Our framework was created not simply by mixing together a bunch of ideas but by conducting research on organizational learning capability and by designing ways to intervene in specific companies to build such capability. Thus our integrated approach is not theory built on theory but was created out of research in real organizations. Our experience in seeing how and why organizations learn led us to a set of overall concepts and practical methods and tools. What we learned is that all organizations have some learning capability that can be described by a set of dimensions we call *Learning Orientations*. Learning is not serendipitous, however. When certain prescriptive conditions that we call *Facilitating Factors* are in place, learning is more apt to occur.

Background

In 1992 we began a research program into the workings of the "learning organization." (The program received initial two-year funding from the International Consortium for Executive Development

Research and administrative support from the Center for Organizational Learning at MIT.) This research evolved through different stages to include an extensive literature review, fieldwork to understand how and why organizations learn, action learning and action research workshops, and the development of tools that help organizations understand and build learning capability.

Among the firms we studied in depth are Centegra Health Systems, Fiat Auto, and Motorola. In workshops and client engagements, we tested our ideas and tools with staff from companies such as AT&T, British Petroleum, Electricité de France (EDF), Exxon Chemical, Merck, Pacific Bell, and Unilever, to name just a few. We continue our research to monitor applications of our ideas, to adapt them to different industries, and to address a series of as yet unanswered questions about organizational learning and corporate performance.

Overview of Contents and Format

By starting with a clear foundation about what organizational learning is and is not, anyone wishing to develop learning capability in their companies and organizations will be able to address the challenge in a consistent fashion. Part One of this book provides that foundation. It describes the various ways learning has been considered in the management literature and presents our framework for understanding how organizations function as learning systems. In particular, it reviews the critical assumptions made by writers about the "learning organization." In lay English, it presents an overview of the thinking about organizational learning and the learning organization. The dominant perspectives are described in Chapter One, followed by a description of our integrated approach in Chapters Two, Three, and Four that combines elements from each perspective.

Examples of organizational learning capability are included as brief case studies in Chapters Three, Four, Five, and Seven. These cases represent organizational learning as it occurred in four distinct settings: two American and two European service and manufacturing settings—Motorola, Mutual Investment Corporation (MIC), Fiat Auto's engineering division (Direzione Technica), and EDF's Exploitation du Parc Nucléaire.

Part Two covers a set of specific learning issues and the implications of our framework. Chapter Five examines how different ways of learning create distinctive organizational learning styles. For example, in some organizations the principal mode of learning leads to incremental, corrective change. Other organizations emphasize learning that produces innovation or transformation. Learning styles should be regarded as a source of core competence and competitive advantage. Though it is important to recognize existing learning capabilities and styles, this book guides practitioners in how to identify desired learning capability. Chapter Six discusses the process of developing a corporate learning strategy. Chapters Seven and Eight provide suggestions on how desired organizational learning capability can be built.

Once a team or organization develops its vision of desired learning capability and takes action to realize that vision, it is important to monitor progress along that path. Chapter Nine addresses the issue of learning assessment and evaluating learning achievements. Much as there is no one way for organizations to learn, so too are there many contexts in which organizations must learn. In Part Three, Chapter Ten considers learning in different industrial contexts and with different types of teams. In particular, we focus on our recent work sponsored by the Healthcare Forum to design learning tools specifically suited to the health care industry. The Conclusion considers the issue of learning outcomes. Management gurus extol the virtues of organizational learning, but what do we know about how learning affects performance? This discussion leads to a broader consideration of the benefit of all this learning: as work teams and organizations become better learners, how, and to what effect, are they using their new capability?

By addressing these questions, we can learn how to make not only our organizations more effective and efficient but perhaps our societies as well. As a species and set of societies based on different cultures, we accumulate knowledge and experience that provide a basis for learning. In some domains the species and its organizations have learned—for example, how to increase food production and how to extract and use fossil fuels. Yet in other domains they have not: we cannot eliminate the toxic wastes our societies create (although we have learned how to move them to out-of-the-way places), nor can we eliminate crime (although we have learned how to put criminals in out-of-the-way places). Why do we learn in some domains but not in others?

We may presume that organizations good at learning will translate that competence into increased productivity and the betterment of society. But what if learning competence is used for exploitative purposes? The spirit behind visions of the learning organization is of personal fulfillment, of win-win scenarios, and of achieving some greater social good. Toward what end or social good is organizational learning capability being directed? What is learned in the companies and organizations that populate our society and economy reflects corporate and social values.

President John F. Kennedy's vision of putting a man on the moon led the U.S. government to support learning in aerospace technology, for example, but in the aftermath many wondered why "we can send a man to the moon, but we can't. . . ." What learning investments are today's organizations making? What learning investment is your company making?

Boston   Anthony J. DiBella
August 1997   Edwin C. Nevis

Acknowledgments

We would like to acknowledge and thank the International Consortium for Executive Development Research (ICEDR) for bringing us together to explore the notion of organizations as learning systems. Their financial support and the guidance provided by Douglas Ready and Joanne Hering gave us the opportunity to conduct our initial research and to test our ideas in workshops with ICEDR members. In particular, we would like to thank three ICEDR member companies—EDF, Fiat, and Mutual Investment Company (a pseudonym)—as well as Motorola, a sponsor of the MIT Center for Organizational Learning, for opening their doors to us and showing us how (and why) organizations learn.

When we began our work together, Janet Gould at MIT was an essential collaborator. Unfortunately, other responsibilities prevented her from contributing to the writing of this book. However, it could not have been written without her contributions as we developed and tested our integrated framework. Thank you, Janet.

In the initial stages of our research, Peter Senge, founder of the Center for Organizational Learning at MIT, gave us a home and provided important logistical support. More recently, through a project supported by the Healthcare Forum, we extended the testing of our methods and tools into the health care industry. There a new set of organizations, including Centegra Health System, Millard Fillmore Health System, and the Sisters of Charity Health Care System, showed us how organizations learn. Our thanks to Wynne Grossman, Susanna Trasolini, and Suzie Haecker for managing that process.

Finally, we would like to acknowledge the support of Cedric Crocker of Jossey-Bass, the skill of Cherie Potts in converting our chicken scratches into legible text, the graphics contributed by Marjorie Ball, and the encouragement of our families and friends, including members of the Boston Consulting Collaborative.

The Authors

ANTHONY J. DIBELLA is president of Organization Transitions, Inc., a consulting firm engaged in applied research and training on learning and change management issues in organizations. He holds a B.A. in sociology from Trinity College (CT), an M.A. in applied anthropology from American University, an M.B.A. from the University of Rhode Island, and a Ph.D. in organization studies from the MIT Sloan School of Management, where he was a visiting scholar at the Center for Organizational Learning. Presently based in Natick, Massachusetts, DiBella has analyzed company operations around the world and consulted with a wide range of organizations, including AT&T, Exxon Chemical, the Healthcare Forum, the National Endowment for the Humanities, Plan International, and the Uganda Central Credit Union. He has taught management at Boston College, MIT, and the University of Massachusetts. He is a codeveloper of the *Organizational Learning Inventory* and the *Healthcare Learning Inventory* and has published on organizational learning, culture, and change in professional and academic journals, including the *Journal of Applied Behavioral Science*, *Journal of Management Studies*, *Sloan Management Review*, and *The Systems Thinker*. For questions or comments on any aspect of this book, DiBella can be reached via the World Wide Web at: http://www.orgtransitions.com or by e-mail at: ajdibella@orgtransitions.com.

EDWIN C. NEVIS recently completed seventeen years at the MIT Sloan School of Management. Starting as a member of the Organization Studies Group, he became director of the Program for Senior Executives. More recently, he served as director of Special Studies of the MIT Center for Organizational Learning, in which capacity he has conducted research in organizational learning.

In addition to his work in executive education, Nevis has practiced organizational consulting for forty years. Since 1973 he has been training consultants in advanced programs. Recently this work has concentrated on working with international consultants engaged in cross-cultural and global change efforts. His book *Organizational Consulting: A Gestalt Approach* has been widely used as a model for this work.

He has been a founder or officer of several successful consulting firms, including Personnel Research & Development Corporation in Cleveland, Ohio. From 1960 to 1972 he was president of the Gestalt Institute of Cleveland, during which time it became a major center for advanced studies by helping professionals. He is also coauthor with Joan Lancourt and Helen Vassallo of *Intentional Revolutions: A Seven-Point Strategy for Transforming Organizations* (1996).

How Organizations Learn

Part I

A Strategic Look
at Organizational Learning

Developing Learning in Organizations

A Matter of Perspective

When we (the authors) began our work together, we looked carefully at what the academic management literature said about how organizations learn and how they become learning organizations. As we read a variety of books and journal article after journal article, we became aware of some common themes and categories. We labeled a set of related themes a "perspective," and with a little nudge here and there it became relatively easy to group authors by one of three perspectives. When we tried to make sense of the confusion and ambiguity in the literature, it helped to use these perspectives to understand what we were reading and to relate it to what we had already read. We also recognized that each perspective had certain strengths and unique ways of looking at or explaining organizational learning and the new phenomenon of the "learning organization."

Our integrated approach builds on the academic management literature in a unique way that is both intellectually compelling and practical (DiBella, 1995). This chapter sets the stage by explaining the three perspectives that provided a foundation for our empirical work and the subsequent design of our integrated approach. Readers knowledgeable of the literature and practitioners with little interest in theoretical distinctions may wish to skip or skim this chapter and proceed directly to the presentation of our framework in Chapter Two.

A Matter of Perspective

There is more than one way to skin a cat, remove snow, design a house, or learn the alphabet. To remove snow, you can use a snowplow, a snow blower, a snow shovel, or your neighbor's kids if you do not have any of your own or if your own are on strike. You could also use snowshoes to simply tramp the snow down rather than remove it, or you could be a snowbird, flying south for the winter and returning after all the snow melts. But if you have never seen snow, you may wonder what all the fuss is about. Indeed, how we deal with most things in our lives depends on how we frame the situation: on our mind-set, our perspective, our point of view—our image, to use Kenneth Boulding's expression (Boulding, 1956)—of the very thing itself. So too with learning and with managers and their consultants who want to build learning organizations. A hammer specialist will see every manager's situation as a nailing problem; a consultant specializing in computerized information management will see the need to build learning organizations as an information technology problem.

What is a learning organization? How can managers make their organizations learning organizations? When turning to these questions, it is important to know the mind-set or perspective of whomever is providing the answers or raising the questions. Depending on who you ask you are apt to get one of three replies based on different assumptions or perspectives about organizations and learning. One response (the *normative perspective*) is that organizational learning only takes place under a unique set of conditions. Another (the *developmental perspective*) is that the learning organization represents a late stage of organization development. A third (the *capability perspective*) presumes that learning is innate to all organizations and that there is no one best way for all organizations to learn. In this chapter we present each of these perspectives and discuss their implications. By understanding the perspective of experts who advocate learning in organizations, we can better understand and thus evaluate their strategies for intervention.

Any manager's course of action for building learning capability in an organization is predicated on some conceptual framework. Whether implicit or explicit, these frameworks reflect assumptions and thinking about organizations and how (or if) they can be controlled. Likewise, theorists and practitioners who have written about learning in organizations have done so on the basis of a set of critical assumptions.

Table 1.1 shows the orientation of various authors in terms of the three principal perspectives about the learning organization. Those listed are an interesting mix of writers whose audience contains both academicians and practitioners. Each orientation is well represented, although the normative perspective has the most adherents.

Table 1.1.   Orientation of Selected Authors

Perspective	Authors
Normative	Garratt (1990)
	Garvin (1993)
	Lessem (1991)
	Mayo and Rick (1993)
	McGill, Slocum, and Lei (1992)
	Pedler, Burgoyne, and Boydell (1991)
	Senge (1990)
	Watkins and Marsick (1993)
Developmental	Argyris and Schön (1978)
	Dechant and Marsick (1991)
	Kimberly (1979)
	Kimberly and Miles (1980)
	Meyers (1990)
	Torbert (1994, 1987)
Capability	Jelinek (1979)
	McKee (1992)
	Nevis, DiBella, and Gould (1993)
	Srivastva (1983)
	Stata (1989)
	Tomassini (1991)
	Wenger (1996)

Before we explain these three perspectives, it is important to differentiate between the similar and related ideas of "organizational learning" and the "learning organization" because they are often used interchangeably. The learning organization is a systems-level concept with particular characteristics or a metaphor for the ideal organization. What do we mean by a systems-level concept? Though companies and organizations are composed of individual employees, they are structured into connected parts, such as departments of marketing, accounting, production, R&D, and the like, that interact as a collection or system of parts to produce a shared, identifiable outcome (profit, number of customers served, or some other indicator of system performance). So on one level there are individual employees, and on another there are employee groups, departments, and functions. A company, firm, or institution also operates at a third level: a systems level that encompasses all the parts that form the whole. Yet no organizational system exists independent of its parts, so when we talk about an organization we ascribe to it characteristics, such as learning, that can only be observed through the actions of the parts.

The learning organization has been characterized as having the capability to adapt to changes in its environment and to respond to lessons of experience by altering organizational behavior. When the price of gasoline increased in the 1970s, for example, American automobile manufacturers reacted by designing smaller and more fuel-efficient cars. Had they learned about such environmental changes sooner they might not have lost as great a share of the new-car market as they did to Japanese manufacturers.

In contrast, "organizational learning" is a term used to describe certain types of activities or processes that may occur at any one of several levels of analysis or as part of an organizational change process. Thus it is something that takes place in all organizations, whereas the learning organization is a particular type or form of organization in and of itself. The two concepts are often used side by side, if not interchangeably, because organizational learning applies to several levels of analysis: individuals learn, teams learn, and companies learn.

The Learning Organization: A Matter of Becoming

One theme in the literature is that organizations may change over time from one or both of two causes. One source of change can be the conscious choices made by managers or that result from other processes internal to the organization. For example, through research and development some organizations behave proactively and create products, such as the home computer or the cellular phone, that spawn new industries or reshape consumer demand. Another source of change derives from intended or unintended adaptations to the environment. When the Volkswagen Beetle became popular in the 1960s, for example, General Motors' response was reactive when it designed and marketed the Corvair, a sporty, rear-engine car.

Another common theme is that organizations do not operate at peak performance but are or should be in a continual state of becoming something more than or different from what they are at present. The implication is that there are dysfunctional aspects of organizations that limit their effectiveness or performance. The role of organizational learning is to help organizations overcome these limits and become something more.

These themes provide a basis for two perspectives. One, the *normative perspective*, views the learning organization as a particular type of organization characterized by a specific set of internal conditions. This perspective presumes that learning organizations do not arise through accident or happenstance but are built from the initiative and strategic choices of key managers. This approach is normative in that it presumes that the learning organization reflects an ideal form and that organizations moving toward it are increasing their chances for organizational success. A second framing, the *developmental perspective*, places the learning organization within the context of an organization's history and its cycle of stages. Here the realization of the learning organization derives as much from evolutionary adaptation to the environment as from revolutionary action based on managerial vision and action.

The Normative Perspective

Some writers presume that learning as a collective activity only takes place under certain conditions or circumstances. Learning, as a mechanism to foster organizational improvement, does not occur through chance or random action but through the development and use of specific skills. Without disciplined action or intervention, organizations fail to learn due to the many forces that constrain learning.

The role of organizational leaders is to create the conditions essential for learning to take place. For example, in his popular writing Peter Senge states that it takes five component technologies or disciplines to establish a learning organization: personal mastery, mental models, shared vision, team learning, and systems thinking. What distinguishes learning organizations is their mastery or focus on these five disciplines. Another normative modeler, David Garvin, claims that learning organizations are skilled at systematic problem solving, experimentation, learning from their own experiences and from others, and transferring knowledge. Other expert prescriptions list openness, systemic thinking, creativity, personal efficacy, and empathy as practices that managers must encourage, recognize, and reward. If these elements are not present, organizations cannot be learning organizations. The "normative" label applies to these approaches because they specify a set of prescriptive conditions, or best practices, that function as a template to evaluate organizations. Organizations that fail to look like or operate like the learning organization (however that is defined) are considered to be suboptimal if not dysfunctional.

Leaders of such organizations are directed to take definitive action that establishes the conditions essential for learning. For example, Garvin (1993, p. 91) claims that although "learning organizations are not built overnight . . . any company that wishes to *become* a learning organization can begin by . . . fostering an environment that is conducive to learning. Another powerful lever is to open up boundaries and stimulate the exchange of ideas . . . and to create learning events." Pedler, Burgoyne, and Boydell (1991, pp. 49–51) list ten action steps that help organizations in "becoming a learning company." Senge (1990, pp. 6–10) explains how building the learning organization is dependent on the establishment of five core disciplines or skills. Managers need to take action so that the profile of their organizations matches the characteristics of the learning organization.

Within the normative perspective there is often a link between learning and organization design. To maximize learning, the design of knowledge work must be formalized and aligned with the influence of decision makers; in effect, becoming a learning organization requires having the right organization structure. For example, Adler and Cole (1993) claim that the work design at NUMMI Motors, the Toyota-GM joint car manufacturing venture, provided greater learning opportunities than did the design of Volvo's Uddevalla plant. Through standardization of work methods, NUMMI could more easily identify problems and areas for improvement that led to learning.

The normative perspective presumes that organizational life is not conducive to learning. Barriers to learning exist due to the fundamental, conflicting ways in which individuals have been trained to think and act and from organizational barriers to discovering and using solutions to organizational problems. For example, Senge claims that organizations do not learn because it is difficult if not impossible to see the consequences of their decisions. The reasons are time lags and the fact that failure is often attributed to conditions in the environment or to factors that cannot be controlled, rather than to internal causes. Becoming a learning organization means that a company must tailor its employees' competences, corporate culture, and formal structures in accordance with the normative conditions. When organizations fail to create these conditions, they suffer from learning disabilities. Normativists have identified a variety of such disabilities, including amnesia (lack of organizational memory), superstition (biased interpretation of experience), paralysis (inability to act), schizophrenia (lack of coordination among organizational constituencies), learned helplessness, truncated learning, and tunnel vision.

To avoid or solve learning disabilities, organizational leadership must establish the normative conditions essential for learning to take place. The focus may be on enhancing the competences of individual members, changing the organizational culture, or redesigning structure. The key is transformative change to create learning possibilities where there had been little or none before. Without the active engagement of its top management, organizations cannot become learning organizations.

The Developmental Perspective

Companies can achieve the status of learning organizations through managerial leadership, but they may also do so through stages of development attained by evolutionary or revolutionary means or both. Organizations are known to develop as a result of their age, size, experience, industry growth, or life cycle (Greiner, 1972; Cameron and Whetten, 1983). One theme in the developmental perspective is that the learning organization represents a phase or stage of an organization's development. Another theme is that the development phase determines the characteristics or style of learning. Learning processes evolve as an organization reaches the later stages in its development as affected by age, growth, management development, or technological innovation.

The learning approach that an organization takes in its infancy evolves into other approaches that are better suited given the accumulation of organizational experience. Learning from action, or enactive learning, is better suited to organizations in their innovating phase. However, learning before action, or proactive learning, is more appropriate for organizations in a mature or routine phase (Kimberly and Miles, 1980).

Meyers (1990) argues that firms pass through five developmental periods in their use of a particular technology and that learning is determined by this life cycle. Mirroring changes in technology, companies progress through cycles of initiation to takeoff, maturity, crisis, and renewal, each with its own dominant mode for learning. According to this perspective, the learning organization operates in a continuous state of becoming as it adjusts to incremental and transformative changes in technology.

Organizations may also be transformed by their own experience of crises and failures. Firms may establish processes to learn incrementally from small failures (Sitkin, 1992) but may also learn from crises or events that are discontinuous with past experience (Weick, 1988). Organizations may reinterpret their own history over time to provide multiple learning opportunities from a single event (March, Sproull, and Tamuz, 1991). For example, business analysts continue to draw lessons from the revitalization of IBM and the demise of Apple Computer. As a people, Americans still try to make sense of their country's experiences in Vietnam, which provides a market for such books as Robert McNamara's pseudo-confessional (1995) on the lessons from Vietnam. What gets learned from such efforts depends on the stage of organization development, the perceived value of information, and the perceived relevance of experience.

In the developmental perspective, firms become learning organizations through the experience of their life cycles. Learning styles and processes vary over time, and the learning organization may be considered the most advanced stage in any organization's development. Within the developmental perspective, organizations may be regarded as evolving in a specific direction where learning processes are adapted, or in a general direction toward the attainment of a stage of maximum adaptability or self-renewal.

The Learning Organization: A Matter of Being

The Capability Perspective

Both the normative and developmental perspectives presuppose that learning is not indigenous to organizational life, that it happens only under certain prescribed conditions, and that it is a goal or vision toward which all organizations should strive. An alternative point of view is to recognize that the concept of a learning organization is as redundant as the notion of a breathing mammal, that organizations as social systems are by their very nature environments in which learning takes place at multiple levels of analysis. This idea provides a foundation for a third perspective on the learning organization. According to the *capability perspective*, organizations do not become learning organizations because learning is an ongoing process. The focus is not on some future vision of becoming a learning organization but on the learning processes that already exist.

Anyone with an MBA degree is familiar with organizational behavior as an area of study; it is commonly a required course. Yet it would be most unusual for any manager to have read about or even heard of the "behaving organization." Why? Because there is a presumption in the discipline of organizational behavior that all organizations, as systems, have behavioral characteristics. Hence talk about the behaving organization would be redundant if not superfluous.

Now consider the notion of the learning organization that suggests that learning and organizations are mutually exclusive. According to the capability perspective, all organizations, as social systems, have learning characteristics. Thus it makes no sense to talk of learning organizations, for that might suggest that there are nonlearning organizations.

Unlike the normative and developmental perspectives, the capability perspective is based on an entirely different set of themes or assumptions about organizations. For example, we know that organizations develop and learn from experience either by strategic choice or by aging. As organizations develop and solve problems of survival, they create a culture that becomes the repository for lessons learned (Schein, 1992). They also create core competences that represent collective learning (Prahalad and Hamel, 1990). Through organizational socialization, a learning process, knowledge and competence are transferred between generations of employees. How new experiences are perceived and how they shape new learning are affected by the simultaneous adaptive capabilities of groups and organizations that exist continuously (Brown and Duguid, 1991).

As all organizations have embedded learning processes, the critical issue is not whether learning takes place or how organizations can become learning organizations. Rather, all organizations are seen as having learning capabilities that embody distinctive styles or patterns of learning; the focal point is understanding what those learning processes are—how, where, and what gets learned. Organizations may not learn at some expert-determined optimal speed, but that does not negate the fact that learning of some sort is always taking place. The key issue is not whether your organization is a learning organization, but what employees learn in your organization and how they learn it. Do employees learn from mistakes or defective merchandise to avoid making them in the future, or do they learn how to avoid letting someone know that a mistake was made in the first place? What are the feedback loops in your organization and what information is fed back? Maybe at your work site colleagues talk less about lessons from work and more about the best places to vacation or where to dine out. Maybe at your work site employees learn more from casual encounters in hallways, bathrooms, elevators, parking lots, and coffee rooms than they do in formal staff meetings. In all these scenarios learning is taking place, although it may not be the type thought to be characteristic of a learning organization.

Within the capability perspective, there is no place for the notion of the learning organization with one set of prescriptive characteristics. For example, the distinction between single-loop learning (learning more about what we already do or know) and double-loop learning (learning about something completely different) is often viewed in normative terms: the latter is necessarily better than the former. But within the capability perspective all approaches have merit; they are simply stylistically different rather than normative or pejorative. Not that all learning behaviors are appropriate in all circumstances. Indeed, under some conditions double-loop or transformative learning would seem to be completely inappropriate. For example, in organizations where performance shortfalls can lead to disaster, transformative learning should be avoided to prevent the potentially dire and unanticipated consequences of operating under a new or experimental set of assumptions. In 1986, Russian engineers at Chernobyl took a transformative approach to learning by trying to generate electricity as a nuclear reactor was being shut down. The tragic results clearly demonstrate the inappropriateness of that form of learning, at least in that context.

The capability perspective represents a pluralistic view toward organizational learning. It assumes that there is no one best way for organizations to learn and that learning processes are embedded in an organization's own culture and structure. The focal point for executives should not be on acquiring the characteristics of the so-called learning organization but on identifying those existent mechanisms whereby learning takes place. For example, organizations may learn from innovative R&D or from production. Bolton (1993) outlined the competitive advantage of learning through imitation versus innovation; Leonard-Barton (1992) recognized the potential for learning from production if factories can be perceived as learning laboratories.

The capability perspective also suggests that different learning styles are apt to be exhibited among the set of organizations that compose any firm. For example, because of the risks involved one would not expect there to be much double-loop or transformative learning taking place in the control room of a nuclear power plant.

However, it would be appropriate for the research and development office in that same utility company to experiment with new designs for nuclear reactors. What management should consider is how the learning styles of the organizations within its firm conflict with or complement one another. Learning styles may differ not only across companies but at different hierarchical levels as well (Jelinek, 1979).

Comparing Perspectives

Table 1.2 shows comparative features of the three perspectives on the learning organization. The developmental perspective is distinct from the normative perspective in that it puts the learning organization within the context of the historical development of

Table 1.2. Three Perspectives on the Learning Organization

| | Perspective | | |
Features	Normative	Developmental	Capability
Time Orientation	Future	Longitudinal	Present
Source	Strategic Action	Evolution, Adaptation	Existence
Learning Style	Unique, Prescribed	Adapted to Stage of Organizational Development	Multiple, Relative
Relationship Between Learning and Culture	Dependence	Parallel in Evolution	Embedded
Management Focal Point	Learning Disabilities	Organizational History	Current Capabilities

the organization as reflected in several criteria. There is an orientation toward longitudinal change and learning through ongoing interpretation of experience. Stage of development shapes an organization's learning style. The normative perspective incorporates a vision for the future with the competences an organization needs to become a learning organization. In both perspectives the learning organization, once achieved, meets the necessary conditions for organizational self-renewal.

According to the capability perspective, the source of learning is organizational existence as revealed through a focus on present behaviors and processes. Here the notion of the learning organization is heresy; all organizations are considered to have learning capabilities. Also, the capability perspective takes a cultural relativist viewpoint by suggesting that no one set of learning styles is better than another.

The relationship between learning and culture is an important distinguishing feature between the three perspectives. In the normative perspective, learning occurs when organizations have the right culture. In the developmental view, as organizations evolve so too does their culture, and from that their learning style. The capability perspective recognizes that organizations are cultures where knowledge about behaviors and values is continually being shared. How such knowledge is shared creates pathways for continuous learning.

Each perspective has different implications for managerial action. The normative perspective presumes that unless the right conditions are present, organizations face barriers to learning; managers must properly diagnose those barriers or "learning disabilities." In contrast, the capabilities perspective, presuming that learning is embedded in culture, directs managers to identify existent processes of learning. In the developmental perspective the focus is not so much on learning but on the organization's stage of development and the process of transition.

Consultants who frame learning in organizations from a normative perspective assume that there is something innately wrong in all organizations that prevents learning from taking place. They see their role as being the outside expert who prescribes what the organization needs in order to remove the learning barriers. In effect, the organization is a sick patient who cannot get better without the doctor's (consultant's) orders. A consultant with a capability perspective would not focus on what is wrong with the organization but on what is right. Instead of assuming the presence of barriers, the consultant would focus on existent learning processes and how knowledge is being acquired, disseminated, and used. A consultant with a developmental framework, however, would not think in terms of what is right or wrong in any absolute sense but in terms of the organization's stage of development. Rather than saying that something is innately wrong or right with the organization, the developmentalist would see everything as a function of the organization's stage of development, such that improving learning capability requires a transition to the next stage.

Managers and practitioners need to recognize that the implications of the three perspectives can be in direct conflict. Yet each perspective contributes in some unique way to our understanding of the learning organization and organizational learning. The normative perspective creates a sense of urgency and vision and provides a clear path for intervention; the developmental perspective points out how context influences learning and reminds us of the need to learn (and relearn) from the past; the capability perspective uncovers the transparency of the present.

The learning organization concept presumes some ability to adapt to change. Management must anticipate or at a minimum recognize new, unanswered questions and problems and use learning skills to solve them. But how do these perspectives on learning in organizations mesh with organization development interventions? A contingency approach for creating organizational learning capability would appear to have merit. For example, for organizations that function in relatively stable environments or that wish to proceed with minimal disruption, the capability perspective provides an appropriate framework for action. When immediate action is considered necessary, the normative perspective affirms the legitimacy for change and provides clear direction. The normative perspective is powerful and appealing to organizations that have no clue where to begin their journey and that seek clear guidance. For example, Peter Senge's latest contribution (Senge and others, 1994) provides practitioners with a wide range of tools and steps to build learning organizations.

The capability perspective appears to be the least threatening, as it does not presume the existence of disabilities that require major change initiatives to rectify. Instead, management focuses on a process of self-discovery and a reaffirmation of existing capabilities. Action research would be an appropriate intervention tool. This approach contributes to an organization's own capability to get better at what it already does.

The presence of these multiple perspectives suggests that the learning organization is, and probably will remain, a chameleon-like target. It means different things to different people. Practitioners should continually assess the meaning and value of the concept. In doing so, they should be cognizant of their own and others' orientations toward learning in organizations and their underlying assumptions about organizations in general. By recognizing the assumptions made by a writer, a reader can more easily comprehend that writer's point of view. It is also easier to see the connections to the works of others and to build a more comprehensive framework that integrates these many paths. The next chapter reveals our way of thinking about and building organizational learning capability that combines the insights of these diverse perspectives.

2

Foundations of an Integrated Strategy

Building organizational learning capability requires clarity about what organizational learning is and how it occurs. Such understanding provides a foundation to guide action and intervention. This chapter explains the foundation and building blocks of our integrated approach: what we learned from our research, how we define organizational learning, and a glimpse at our overall framework and how it relates to the organizational learning cycle.

What We Learned About Learning

Insight from the three dominant perspectives (normative, developmental, capability) on learning in organizations suggests that to build learning capability requires addressing three major needs:

> *Need to enhance factors that promote learning.* We know that most learning is not the outcome of mere serendipity but requires specific effort and focused action. The normative approach also suggests that some innate conditions of organizational life are detrimental to organizational learning. In effect, some factors promote learning and others create barriers to it. An integrated approach needs to include those "best practices" that promote learning.

Need to provide a mechanism for change and development of learning styles and capabilities. Organizations are not static but are subject to ongoing change and adaptation. The developmental perspective suggests that as organizations mature their learning capabilities evolve. To do so, specific action must be taken to alter or adapt an organization's culturally patterned ways of learning.

Need to depict in a descriptive way how learning takes place. As the learning process functions in all organizational settings, an integrated approach must somehow depict these ongoing processes. In effect, we need a way to profile how organizations learn. The result should be a cultural ethnography that describes the innate learning capabilities of all organizations.

By pooling the insights from the three perspectives, we can generate a more complete understanding of what it takes to build organizational learning capability. With a sense of these needs or pieces, we studied several organizations to understand exactly how and why they learned. At Motorola, we studied two teams of senior managers drawn from all parts of the company. At Mutual Investment Corporation, we studied the marketing department and a group of fund managers. The other two sites were Nuclear Power Operations at Electricité de France and the engineering division of Fiat Automobile. Vignettes of learning at these organizations are included throughout the following chapters. Four core themes emerged from this research.

All Organizations Are Learning Systems

All the sites we studied have formal and informal processes and structures in place for the acquisition, sharing, and utilization of knowledge and skills. In this sense, organizations can be thought of as learning systems. Values, norms, procedures, and business performance data are communicated broadly and assimilated by members, starting with early socialization and continuing through all types of group communications, both formal and informal. In some firms we talked with staff who claimed that their companies were not good learning organizations, but in each instance we were able to identify one or more core competences that could only have come into existence if there were learning investments in those areas. There would have to be some type of structure or process to support the informed experience and formal educational interventions required for learning to take place. And indeed that is what we found in our field sites and other firms. For example, one firm that considers itself to be a poor learning organization because of some learning disabilities has a reputation in its industry for its superior field marketing function. In looking at this firm it is clear that it has well-developed recruiting, socialization, training and development, and rotational assignment practices that support a continually filled cadre of respected marketing people. Such practices engender learning and the assimilation of culture in a significant way.

Learning Conforms to Organizational Culture

The nature of learning and the way it takes place are determined in large measure by the culture of the organization. For example, the entrepreneurial nature of Mutual Investment Corporation's Investment Funds Group (MIC-IFG) results in a learning approach in which considerable amounts of information are made available to fund managers and analysts but the use of that information remains at the discretion of the managers. In addition, there is a good deal of leeway as to how fund managers make their investment decisions; some are intuitive, some rely heavily on historic performance, and a few use computer programs of some sophistication. The utilization or application of learning among fund managers is largely an informal process, not one dictated by formal firmwide programs. These processes are consistent with MIC's corporate culture, which values independent decision making and entrepreneurial spirit.

The findings at Motorola are illuminating in a different way. There is no question that a great deal of organizational learning about quality has occurred in the firm, but the emphasis on engineering and technical concerns resulted in a much earlier and complete embrace of the total quality quest by discrete product manufacturing groups than by other functions. In a culture that heavily rewards product group performance, total quality in products that require integrated, intergroup action lags behind, particularly in the marketing of systems that cut across divisions.

Stylistic Variations in Organizational Learning

Organizations attempt to create and maximize their learning in various ways. Basic assumptions in a culture lead to learning values and to select investments in different aspects of the business. This produces a learning style that will be different from one with another pattern of values and investments. These variations in style are based on a series of Learning Orientations (dimensions of learning) that may or may not be consciously perceived by members of the organization. As an example of these factors, each of two distinct groups at both Motorola and MIC had a different approach to the way knowledge and skills were accrued and utilized. In one of the Motorola groups there was a great deal of concern for specifying the metrics that would be used to define and measure the targeted learning. In the other, there was much less concern with very specific measures; instead, broad objectives were stressed. In the two groups at MIC the methods for sharing and utilizing knowledge were very different. Among investment funds staff information sharing was informal, but among marketing staff it was more formal and collaborative. From these variations, we concluded that the pattern of the Learning Orientations is a large part of what makes up an organizational learning system. It may not tell us how well learning is promoted, but it does tell us a great deal about what is learned and where learning takes place.

Learning Is Facilitated by Several Generic Processes

How well an organization maximizes learning within its chosen style is not a haphazard matter. There is a normative aspect to our research findings that suggests that the concept of the "learning organization" is partially correct: some policies, structures, and processes do make a difference. The difference is in how easy or hard it is for useful learning to occur and in how effective the organization is in "working its style." Though we did not see all these factors in each of the six sites we studied intensively, we did see most of them and we do see them in other sites. Thus we are prepared to view them as generic factors, those that any organization can benefit from regardless of its learning style. For example, scanning, in which benchmarking plays an important role, was so central to the learning at Motorola that it is now an integral, ongoing aspect of every important initiative in the company. Although MIC tends to create knowledge and skill internally, it maintains an ongoing vigilance with regard to its external environment.

Our Framework

Our research indicated that developing learning capability requires an ability to describe how learning occurs and what gets learned and to evaluate characteristics that promote organizational learning.

Based on these implications, we developed a two-part framework of organizational learning capability. One part is composed of *Learning Orientations* that represent the ways learning takes place and the nature of what is learned. These orientations can form patterns that define a given organization's learning style. In this sense, they are elements that help us understand learning processes in a descriptive manner. The second part of our framework is composed of *Facilitating Factors*, the structures and actions that affect how easy or hard it is for learning to occur and the amount of effective learning that takes place. These are normative elements based on the best practices in dealing with generic issues. Both types of elements are required to understand an organization's learning capability. Figure 2.1 shows how the two parts of our framework may be depicted.

Altogether we identified seven Learning Orientations and ten Facilitating Factors that are described at length in the next two chapters. This set of seventeen elements provides a way to profile an organization's learning capability. By recognizing existing although perhaps transparent capabilities, work teams and organizations can acknowledge the present and use that awareness as a takeoff point for building desired learning capability. The two-part integrated framework provides multiple ways to build capability. For example, an organization may change what it is learning by shifting its Learning Orientations or improve the quality of its learning through better performance on the Facilitating Factors.

Some readers may wish to proceed directly to Chapters Three and Four for a detailed explanation of the seven Learning Orienta-

Figure 2.1.   The Two Parts of Organizational Learning Capability

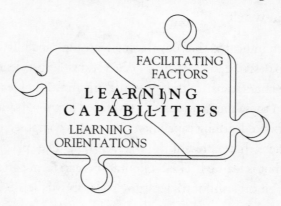

Learning Orientations

- Describe how learning occurs and what is learned
- Based on culture and core competence

Facilitating Factors

- Specify elements that promote learning
- Based on "best practices" and common processes

tions and ten Facilitating Factors. However, other curious readers may wish to explore a few other pieces in our foundation: What do we mean by organizational learning? What is the organizational learning cycle?

What Makes Organizational Learning Organizational

Learning is easily understood in its general meaning; anyone who has gone to school or heard a parent's teachings knows what learning is. However, when we work with others to develop programs or policies on learning, we find many different interpretations of what learning really is. Also, when talking of organizational learning, we obviously mean something other than the schooling of our children or employees, but what?

Our interest in learning is focused on organizations, not individuals. Hence it is important to avoid the attractiveness of anthropomorphism, the act of attributing human or personal characteristics to what is not human. We should not take a definition of learning suited to individuals and apply it to organizations. Instead we need to recognize how organizational learning differs from the learning of individuals.

There are three essential criteria of organizational learning:

First, *new skills, attitudes, values, and behaviors are created or acquired over time*. Life is like a river, ever-flowing, ever-changing. With changes in technology, demographics, and consumer preferences, new ways of thinking and behaving are continually being created from our own experiences and the experiences of others. One context for this type of change is organizations where experiences with customers, production mishaps, or marketing breakthroughs provide opportunities to create new knowledge or insight. Learning is the conversion of such experiences into new skills, attitudes, values, behaviors, or products.

Doing the same thing in the same way in the same frame of mind does not represent learning. To say that learning has occurred means that something has changed—if not behavior, then how we think about what we do or how we feel about it. Sometimes change will occur before we are even aware of it, which is why we can talk about organizational learning. Unlike individuals, organizations lack consciousness, but this does not mean that organizations cannot learn. Awareness of something learned may come after the fact.

Second, *what is learned becomes the property of some collective unit.* Organizational learning is a social process whereby some insight or knowledge, created either by an individual working alone or by a team, becomes accessible to others. This process occurs in an organization—a recognizable set of work groups, departments, or units—where the interaction of its members produces some definable outcome. Organizational learning is not about how individuals, as individuals, learn in an organization, but about how individuals and work groups working with others learn from one another's experience. Organizational learning has distinctive meaning because it separates the learning of an individual from the patterned learning that occurs in a group. When individuals work together, their collective behavior forms patterns or configurations often referred to as "how things are done around here." Some of this behavior pertains to how learning takes place and what members of the group learn. Thus we can talk both about the distinctive learning competence of a group of individuals working together and about what the group learns over time. Both components—what is learned and how learning takes place—are properties of the group.

Third, *what is learned remains within the organization or group even if individuals leave.* The proof of this distinctive competence of groups is that what has been learned remains even when members of the group leave. This is the third criterion of organizational learning. When employees of a firm leave, the firm loses an asset: access to that employee's time and talent. For example, losing employees to retirement, relocation, or other employers is inevitable, but because they take their expertise with them the firm loses more than a warm body, it loses lessons from experience. Thus it may need to reinvent the wheel or repeat history before the employee's competence is again available to it. Firms and organizations that are unable to retain experience must reinvest resources to regain the competence that is lost when learning on an organizational level does not occur. For organizations with poor learning capability, using downsizing as a management technique can have very high long-term costs. Often the staff let go in a downsizing are those who have been with the company the longest and are the highest paid but also the most experienced. Companies need to consider what they are losing in accrued learning when they lay off or downsize experienced staff. A few years ago we worked with a large international organization that went through a downsizing of its headquarters staff. This organization had done little to capture the expertise of its staff, so when its most senior and (some felt) most competent staff left, the director of human resources told us that "our collective memory is walking out the door." For this organization and others like it, downsizing meant the loss of learning.

The three criteria of organizational learning are important to note because collectively they indicate why learning is important. Learning is about gaining experience, building competence, and avoiding the repetition of mistakes, problems, and errors that waste resources. Mistakes and errors may not be critical in themselves and may result from unforeseen circumstances, but our failure to learn from them or their recurrence is problematic. America's space program, for example, was built on the foundation of past successes and failures.

Many experts, including David Garvin, Ed Schein, and Peter Senge, define organizational learning as an organization's ability to adapt to change. Our notion of learning goes beyond adaptation as an organization's response to changing external circumstances. Factors in our immediate (internal as opposed to external) environment change from time alone and from the experience we have over time. Learning involves how we process that experience. For as long as our organizations function, experience is unending and hence so is learning.

We define organizational learning as *the capacity or processes within an organization to maintain or improve performance based on experience*. With change being a constant in today's society, we must move, act, and react simply to stay in the same place. So too with learning. We must remain knowledgeable about our environments just to maintain our present situation, and to improve our competitiveness we must learn even faster. It is like being in a howling, eighty-mile-an-hour hurricane: to avoid being thrown backward we must expend a lot of effort to fight the wind. A person observing our action from the comfort of a house might attribute our lack of relative movement to our lack of effort even as we strain to stay in the same place!

Today, companies must learn just to keep up with what is going on around them. This process becomes transparent over time, as we are bound by relativity: if a company's pace of learning is the same relative to its environment, then it can appear that the organization is not learning. In today's business environment, often described as turbulent, companies must learn and change just to stay in the same place. That is why learning is important and why we cannot escape from it.

Learning as a Cycle of Three Processes

Building on the work of George Huber (1991), we conceive of organizational learning as a series of three processes: Knowledge Creation or Acquisition, Knowledge Dissemination, and Knowledge Use (see Figure 2.2). To say that learning has occurred means that new knowledge has come into an organizational system, has been disseminated or transferred, and is or was used. Organizational learning requires all three processes in the cycle. Unless new knowledge is disseminated or shared, it remains the property of individuals rather than the organization at large (see the second criterion just presented). As property of the organization, it is accessible and used at some level; at a minimum, new knowledge changes one's view of the world.

Figure 2.2.   The Organizational Learning Cycle

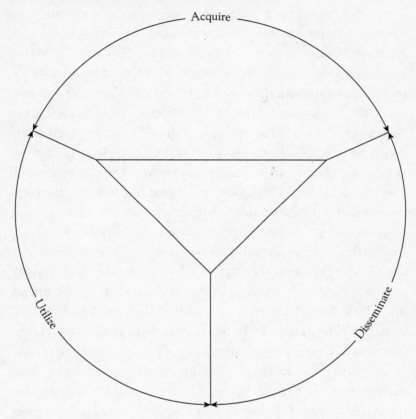

Source: Nevis, DiBella, and Gould, 1995.

Knowledge Creation or Acquisition

Organizations gain knowledge directly through the experiences of their own employees or indirectly through the experiences of other organizations. Hence the first phase of the learning cycle may involve either the creation or acquisition of knowledge. As social systems in which employees are continually generating experiences, organizations can potentially be learning all the time, in which case learning becomes endemic to the organization.

In order to recognize what is special about learning, it is important to distinguish between information and knowledge. We generate knowledge when we give meaning to information or experience. For the learning cycle to be engaged, employees must give meaning to information so that the creation of knowledge provides a basis for action. It is not sufficient to have the information in the system; organizational members must have a shared basis for interpreting that information and giving it meaning. When this does not occur, the learning cycle breaks down, which can lead to tragic consequences. An excellent example is the 1990 plane crash of an Avianca flight from Miami to New York. Due to inclement weather, the Avianca flight had been delayed several times as it proceeded north from Florida. Throughout the flight, the cockpit crew kept informing FAA flight traffic controllers how many hours of fuel remained. To the Avianca crew, that meant literally the amount of time before the plane's fuel supply was used up. Unfortunately, to the FAA staff it meant the number of hours of fuel remaining *above* the plane's FAA safety threshold. As the Avianca flight was guided up to New York, flight traffic controllers thought the plane had enough fuel to land. In fact, the Avianca flight crashed on a Long Island hillside when the plane ran out of fuel on its final approach to John F. Kennedy International Airport. The critical information necessary to have averted this incident was available, but there was no shared knowledge. The lack of shared knowledge prevented FAA staff from recognizing the vulnerability of the ill-fated Avianca flight.

Since organizations are continually creating experience and thus creating or acquiring knowledge, the potential for learning is always there. To realize that potential, organizations must have the capacity to disseminate and use that knowledge. It is important to distinguish between the capacity of organizations to produce, disseminate, and use knowledge and the content of exactly what is being learned. One way to understand this distinction is to ask what knowledge is being produced, acquired, or disseminated in your organization. For example, what do company staff talk about when they gather by the coffee machine or formally at staff meetings? When staff meet outside the office, as at Christmas parties or company barbecues, what knowledge do they exchange? When staff mingle, there are endless possibilities about what they can discuss: sports (the Olympics, the Super Bowl, or the Tour de France), current world events (terrorist bombings in the Middle East or the love lives of the British royal family), or "shop talk" (who has been hired, who may get fired, who has the CEO's ear, who is in and who is out, what new products R&D is working on, quarterly sales figures). The information and knowledge that staff share provide a basis for learning and change, although staff don't learn simply because information is available.

In giving meaning to information and making it knowledge, staff often consider the sources of such information, be it rumor, research report, or recognized expert. Understanding the learning process at an organizational level means focusing not only on what information is being shared among staff but where the information comes from and who is doing the sharing. The utilization of knowledge depends not only on its perceived relevance but its social legitimacy as well. Recently we worked with a health services firm that had implemented a program in total quality management (TQM). One outcome was an increased awareness of and sensitivity to customer needs and perceptions. When TQM staff learned about customer complaints, they quickly responded and worked with clinicians to rectify any shortcomings in service. This feedback system was a productive way to learn about the firm's experiences to make service improvements, but it had a hidden cost: so much effort was made to respond to customer complaints about service that when staff complained about deficiencies their concerns went unheeded. It was easier to avoid staff knowledge about service deficiencies than it was to ignore customers' complaints. The point is that the contribution of knowledge to learning will depend on who is the source of the knowledge in the first place.

Beyond considering the source of knowledge, it is important to recognize *how* the knowledge was generated and came to be part of the organization's knowledge system. Some firms, such as WalMart, conduct ongoing in-store experiments in packaging and pricing to learn better ways of satisfying their customers. Procter & Gamble is known not only for its marketing research to solicit customers' desires and needs but also for its product development labs, where ideas for new products take shape. Knowledge can enter a firm's learning cycle through formal mechanisms to scan the experiences of customers, suppliers, competitors, or industry trends.

Beyond the question of how knowledge is captured or created lies the related issues of why, where, and when it is captured or created. These issues can best be understood if a firm has clearly defined what a learning opportunity is and developed processes to generate knowledge from such events. For example, to the National Transportation Safety Board (NTSB) any crash of a civilian aircraft, commercial or private, is treated as a learning opportunity. Immediately after the NTSB is notified of a crash it sends out a team of investigators to understand why the crash occurred and what implications it might have for such factors as plane design, maintenance, air traffic control procedures, or flight crew training. Investigatory teams often consist of personnel from the aircraft manufacturer, engine designer, or airline company. Company representatives get involved not only because the NTSB can use their expertise but because their companies must often participate in the set of corrective actions necessary to avoid the recurrence of such crashes. Each year far more people die from automobile accidents than plane accidents, but unlike in the civilian aviation industry, more auto safety lessons are generated from formal experiments and tests with passenger dummies than from real car crashes. Learning occurs at the NTSB because crashes and accidents clearly define what a learning opportunity is and because the failure to learn from each event can have disastrous consequences.

Knowledge Dissemination

One way to think about the dissemination of knowledge and its role in the learning cycle comes from the distinction between tacit knowledge and explicit knowledge (Nonaka, 1991). *Tacit knowledge* pertains to personal insights, intuitions, and abilities; *explicit knowledge* pertains to knowledge that can be shared and communicated. In organizations knowledge is openly disseminated through a variety of ways or channels. One result is that knowledge, which at one time was very personal or tacit, is shared and becomes available to others in the organization. As employees gain experience and presumably expertise, firms need processes to transmit those experiences. Some of these processes can be very formal, others informal. For example, consider the function of exit interviews with departing staff. How many firms make an effort to glean from departing staff what they have learned about the company's work and how best to handle their job responsibilities? Unless the tacit knowledge of such employees is converted and disseminated, it will not be retained as part of the firm's competence. Exit interviews are a formal way to disseminate knowledge and engage the organizational learning cycle. Unfortunately, in too many firms, when employees give notice or are asked to vacate their positions, they quickly become part of the firm's history. No provision is made to capture for the firm what the employee knows about the business or about his or her job responsibilities. This failure creates a precondition for the "reinventing the wheel" syndrome whereby new employees, hired at lower salaries, repeat the lessons already learned by their predecessors. This problem is particularly acute in professional occupations and service industries where work is rarely proceduralized and competence comes from tacit knowledge.

Knowledge can be disseminated within an organization and between employees in a variety of other ways. For example, consider the function of the following media:

Staff newsletters

Productivity reports

Industrial accident or incident reports

Computerized management information systems

Staff training seminars

CEO speeches

Staff conferences

E-mail

Voice-mail

Telephone

Skits, plays, dramatic reenactments

Special events

Some modes of dissemination are more formal than others; some are based on written communications (formal reports and documents, for example), others on oral presentation (staff presentations and telephone conversations, for example).

To engage the learning cycle, some firms move their employees instead of their knowledge. Consider, for example, the role of a job rotation or career development system. These human resource systems are processes of organizational learning, for they result in staff moving around to different functions or levels of decision making. The expectation is that such movement will allow staff to learn from one another. When knowledge in one area of the firm is disseminated to a rotating staff member, it can subsequently be disseminated to another area of the firm when the employee is relocated.

The timing of knowledge sharing and its impact on how that knowledge is used is another aspect of knowledge dissemination. For example, does knowledge that could be perceived as bad news travel any faster than what might be considered good news? When a staff layoff occurs, knowledge about who is to be included can have a debilitating effect on staff morale. According to outplacement specialists, it is better to share that information on Monday rather than Friday; if done on Friday the staff have all weekend to worry about the implications, read the employment ads in their Sunday newspaper, and mail out a few résumés by Monday.

Speed of knowledge dissemination can also be influenced by who is doing the dissemination, the implications of the knowledge being transmitted, and the spatial design of offices. For example, cubicles increase visual contact between staff with the expectation that it will also increase verbal communication as compared with an office design that emphasizes private offices with thick doors that can be locked. Several years ago, Apple Computer designed its new headquarters building in an open format to maximize staff interaction and the dissemination of knowledge. The new design was consistent with the traditional corporate culture at Apple that values innovation and informality. The impact of culture on corporate communications and knowledge dissemination can be seen across national borders as well. For example, although the French value their privacy as much as Americans and provide their executives with their own offices, French firms also have coffee bars where staff congregate after lunch to share knowledge.

Whether knowledge is disseminated in an organization depends also on the outcome of doing so. The expression "knowledge is power" suggests that tacit knowledge will not readily be shared. Employees may fear that by sharing knowledge their employer will be less dependent on them. Firms need to engender values that will produce exactly the opposite feeling. By sharing knowledge employees can demonstrate their contribution to organizational learning, and firms need to recognize such employees. Business programs that reward staff for innovative ideas or ways to reduce costs or increase productivity support organizational learning behavior. Another form of knowledge dissemination is characterized by "open-book management" (Case, 1995), which advocates the sharing of knowledge that is customarily accessible only to top management or investors. Corporations must furnish shareholders with detailed financial statements and information on corporate strategies on an annual or quarterly basis, and open-book management suggests that such information regularly be shared with employees as well.

Knowledge Use

Knowledge may be generated and disseminated throughout an organization, but unless it is used to alter our decisions, our behavior, or
our culture then the learning cycle remains incomplete. The break-
down of the learning cycle at this stage is exhibited in many historical cases. In 1941, for example, after breaking the code for
Japanese transmissions, U.S. government officials knew that a
Japanese attack on an American base in the Pacific was imminent.
Yet they took no action, enabling the "surprise" attack on Pearl
Harbor. In 1986, when NASA officials were faced with the decision
about whether to launch the *Challenger* space shuttle, they had
knowledge about the probable failure of the O-rings; engineers at
Morton-Thiokol had produced that knowledge and disseminated it
to NASA. Unfortunately, it took the explosion of the *Challenger* for
learning to occur. In 1993, officials of the Bureau of Alcohol,
Tobacco, & Firearms (ATF) of the U.S. Justice Department received word that David Koresh and his followers were well-armed
and preparing a "surprise" response to ATF's visit to their compound
in Waco, Texas. They ignored that knowledge, leading to the death
of four ATF agents and the wounding of more than a dozen. Examples of the nonuse of knowledge also exist in the world of business.
In the 1970s, for example, Ford officials realized the danger of the
location of fuel tanks on their Pinto models but took no action to
redesign the car.

How or if knowledge is used reflects our values and indicates
preferences for certain outcomes. It could be argued that Ford knew
about the Pinto's fuel tank problem but chose to do nothing because
it considered that the most cost-effective response. When knowledge is created and disseminated around an organization, it can
challenge our view of the world and point out the need for change.
Whether we use that knowledge to alter our course depends on a
variety of factors that together compose the relative cost of learn-

ing. Although it is easy to talk of the benefits of learning, we need to realize that learning comes at a cost; when that cost is considered to be too high, what has been learned will not be used.

If learning was that innately advantageous, there would be no problem in completing the learning cycle. To counter the costs of learning, companies must establish mechanisms to use organizational experience. Motivational and incentive systems can support the assimilation and use of knowledge by providing positive or negative reinforcements. For example, what encouragement is provided to staff to ensure that information from internal operations and performance is analyzed and used? How are new work processes assimilated?

A critical question is whether our organizations are learning what they should be learning. For example, on the first day of work a new employee may acquire a wide range of knowledge, including where fellow employees have lunch, who eats with whom, and whether staff take coffee breaks and for how long. Staff may use such knowledge to find ways of fitting in and getting accepted, but what of knowledge about how to perform work in the most efficient manner? Is that knowledge acquired and used?

The depiction of the organizational learning cycle provides a generic, integrated basis for understanding organizational learning capability. While claiming that organizations have processes to acquire, disseminate, and use knowledge, we need to be aware that these processes may be used for outcomes other than those desired by an organization's leadership. For example, instead of learning from one another how to be more productive, staff may instead focus on learning how to avoid managerial direction. To ensure that the content of the learning process generates specific results requires deliberate effort.

Each phase of the organizational learning cycle can be described or improved on the basis of our integrated approach. Our research suggests that certain Learning Orientations and Facilitating Factors are most relevant to certain portions of the learning cycle. Figure 2.3 shows a mapping of the seventeen elements in our integrated approach with the learning cycle. Three elements are set in the center of the figure, as they help develop all phases of the learning cycle. The next two chapters explain all the elements in depth.

Figure 2.3. Elements in Our Integrated Approach Mapped Onto the Learning Cycle

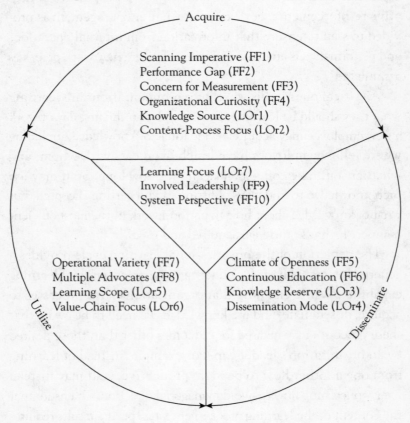

LOr = Learning Orientation
FF = Facilitating Factor

Source: An earlier version appeared in Nevis, DiBella, and Gould, 1995, p. 82.

3

How Organizations Learn
Learning Orientations

The first section of our integrated framework consists of Learning Orientations (LOrs) that reflect how learning takes place and the content of learning. Organizations make all kinds of choices with regard to what is important to learn and how they will do so. Although making learning investment decisions is generally not seen as a management task, management strategies always carry an implicit choice about learning. For example, if a firm decides that it will define itself as producing the best-engineered product in its industry, it follows that a significant amount of planning, analysis, and resources (money and people) will be devoted to this objective. Attention will be paid to learning from the experience that emerges in implementing this decision. It is likely that more money will be made available for this, and less to manufacturing and marketing the product. This chapter explains how learning choices can be described.

Describing Learning Choices

LOrs represent the practices by which knowledge is acquired, disseminated, or used. They are defined in terms of opposite approaches that represent a critical learning process. As descriptive elements, they are represented as paired contrasts or approaches situated along a continuum. A learning approach represents an extreme position on a continuum. Learning occurs all along each continuum; there is no right or wrong location along one. For every LOr, organizations might use some mix of both approaches but may prefer one over another.

For example, our data revealed multiple sources for the knowledge disseminated within organizations. Some organizations acquire knowledge from their external environment; others generate or create knowledge internally. Many rely on both to varying degrees. Electricité de France (EDF), for example, acquires a significant amount of knowledge internally from its management of fifty-six nuclear power plants of similar design. Knowledge gained from operating these plants is used to make corrections and develop lessons about how to improve performance. However, EDF concurrently acquires knowledge via the International Atomic Energy Agency about the performance of nuclear power plants throughout the world. This source of knowledge complements EDF's internal sources. (EDF, in fact, learned a great deal from the nuclear accident at Three Mile Island in the United States.) Thus, with regard to EDF it is not sufficient to say that its knowledge source is internal or external, for it is a combination of both, and this can be represented by a continuum of emphasis from "extremely internal" to "extremely external." In similar fashion, we identified six other orientations to learning that characterize how learning takes place.

Following is a summary of the principal characteristics of Learning Orientations:

- Reflect where and how knowledge is acquired, disseminated, or used

- Represent what is learned or considered important to learn

- Indicate where a work group or team makes its learning investments

- Are bipolar continuums of two contrasting approaches

- Determine learning style

Here are definitions of the seven Learning Orientations:

1. *Knowledge Source*. Preference for developing knowledge internally versus preference for acquiring knowledge developed externally

2. *Content-Process Focus*. Emphasis on knowledge about *what* products or services are as compared to emphasis on knowledge about *how* those products or services are developed or delivered

3. *Knowledge Reserve*. Knowledge possessed by individuals as compared to knowledge that is publicly available

4. *Dissemination Mode*. Knowledge shared in formal, prescribed methods as compared to knowledge shared through informal methods, such as role modeling and casual interaction

5. *Learning Scope*. Preference for knowledge related to the improvement of existing capabilities, products, or services as compared to preference for knowledge related to the development of new ones

6. *Value-Chain Focus*. Emphasis on learning investments in engineering or production activities ("design-and-make" functions) versus sales or service ("market-and-deliver" functions)

7. *Learning Focus*. Development of knowledge pertaining to individual performance as compared to the development of knowledge pertaining to group performance

Figure 3.1 portrays how each LOr can be visualized along a continuum of two extreme approaches. The balance of this chapter explains each of the seven LOrs and gives examples. The order of

Figure 3.1.   Learning Orientation Continuums

Name	Approach	
1. Knowledge Source	internal	external
2. Content-Process Focus	content	process
3. Knowledge Reserve	personal	public
4. Dissemination Mode	formal	informal
5. Learning Scope	incremental	transformative
6. Value-Chain Focus	design-make	market-deliver
7. Learning Focus	individual	group

the seven LOrs is based on their position in the learning cycle. At the end of this chapter is a brief description of how learning occurs at EDF, one of the sites we studied in depth.

Knowledge Source

This orientation is defined as the extent to which an organization prefers to develop new knowledge internally versus externally. This distinction is often thought of as the difference between innovation and adaptation or imitation, or between preferring to be first to market rather than a "market follower." For those who want to be first to market, the goal is to invest in proprietary new products and take early advantage of a window of opportunity. A market follower instead learns by observing what has been developed by others and makes a modification or "value-added" addition designed to capture a piece of a market created by others or to expand the market.

In the United States there has been a tendency to value the innovative approach more highly and to look down on those who seem to be copiers. American critiques of Japanese businesses often mention the Japanese as being good imitators but not good innovators. We see both of these approaches as having great merit, as stylistically opposite choices rather than as normative strategies. In a well-argued paper, Bolton (1993) makes a distinction between learning by doing (innovation) and learning by watching (imitation). She breaks imitation into two varieties: pure imitation and reflective imitation. Pure imitation is the "unchewed" introjection of an idea and results in a low level of learning because there is no enriched ground on which to build new knowledge. Reflective imitation requires active adaptation of knowledge to a new setting and requires real work to assimilate a new possibility.

Bolton shows the competitive advantages of both innovation and reflective imitation, indicating that Japanese successes have come from the latter. However, this does not imply an issue of different national cultures. One need only look at how IBM used reflective imitation some fifty years ago to take what Univac had innovated—a computer's central processing unit—and gained domination of the field by better implementation of the concept. Likewise, Toyota capitalized on the groundbreaking work done by Honda, entering markets later but staking out a significant place. And the world is populated by products and businesses built on seeing opportunity in the products of research at Bell Labs.

The implications of a value choice in this LOr are important. Choosing to use internally developed knowledge on the assumption that it is the source of competitive advantage is to decide to invest heavily in one's own research and development. It is to decide that the organization can learn heavily from its own experiences and that investment in a "research learning curve" will reap handsome dividends. Conversely, to choose to emphasize external knowledge is to decide to make a heavy investment in environmental scanning or ways of evaluating what others are doing. To do it well also involves an investment in learning to produce what others design, perhaps to learn how to be a low-cost producer. Each decision leads to different deployment of resources, and both choices can be made to work well. The issue is whether a firm understands fully that it does have a preference and recognizes that making this preference work well involves significant learning.

Our research shows a tendency for organizations to prefer one approach (internal or external Knowledge Source) over the other. For example, MIC does a good job of scanning its environment but prefers to innovate in responding to needs and problems; it has been a leader in coming up with new products and services. EDF modeled its network of nuclear power plants on American technology. Motorola is interesting in that it appears to be equally vigorous in innovating and in reflective imitation. It has been very innovative in developing new products but also very adroit in adapting processes developed by others, such as benchmarking and TQM procedures.

We can also see differences in these preferences in well-known companies. American Airlines, WalMart, Merck, Daimler Benz, 3M, and Rubbermaid appear to be heavily internally oriented in producing knowledge, tending to be first to market and to invest heavily in internal research. American Home Products is a good example of a reflective imitator that has managed to achieve consistent success with less investment in R&D than the most successful pharmaceutical firms. Another recent, highly successful imitation was the development of the AT&T Universal Card. In many ways the credit card market was mature. Yet AT&T combined its vast databank of names with its expertise in processing invoices, granted charter card holders a lifetime exemption from annual fees, and within a few years became one of the top four firms in credit card accounts. A further example is Tyco Toys, which studied Lego and found a way to develop a competing product that achieved a large market share. Still others can be found in how the Lexus and Infiniti automobiles were inspired by the way Mercedes Benz had become the foremost maker of luxury cars.

Thus we see that organizations use more than one source of knowledge to learn. The challenge for an organization is to consider both approaches, to see which it does well, and to decide if it is comfortable with its balance of approaches. An important issue is to determine whether to build in the best possible way on what already exists or to attempt a transformation. Later we will look at implementation issues for these choices.

Content-Process Focus

This Learning Orientation refers to a preference for knowledge related to the definition of products or services as opposed to knowledge about the basic processes that might underlie or support them. On the one hand is a strong focus on the deliverables themselves; on the other is a focus on core capabilities that can be applied to the task of developing or delivering them. Each is important to organizational effectiveness, but we find that few organizations have invested fully in both. Many observers have stated that one of the reasons the Japanese became so competitive is that they made considerable investment in process technologies, unlike U.S. firms during the 1960s and 1970s. For example, American automobile and consumer electronic companies led the way in concept, content, and design of their products, but the Japanese adapted these and learned processes to achieve better outcomes. As Hamel and Prahalad (1994) noted, Canon developed great strength in eight core processes that resulted in thirty different products. Since the mid-1970s U.S. firms have shifted their focus considerably, as seen in the growth of Total Quality Management and Business Process Reengineering, both of which are heavily concerned with process improvement.

The distinction noted here is of special importance to service businesses and service and support groups within a company. We can think of services as specialized process providers, but these groups provide a product. Thus a consulting firm that provides analytic services to clients needs to acquire knowledge about the processes it uses in its analysis, the processes that hold the business together, and the deliverables—usually written or oral reports. Common sense dictates that both content and process are important, yet in observing many such groups or firms we notice significant variations in preference. Many professional firms concentrate so heavily on the content of their deliverables that they are almost blind about process improvement learning. As a consequence, the product is delivered later or at greater expense than necessary, or with avoidable stress on the professionals involved.

In the organizations we studied there are significant variations. Electricité de France's Nuclear Power Operations, as might be expected, makes heavy investment in knowledge about its processes. Historically, the Investment Funds Group of MIC has been heavily focused on content or product development; only in recent years has it paid more attention to process improvement learning. The same is true of Fiat Auto's Direzione Technica. Motorola shows evidence of making learning investments in both approaches in this LOr: executives we observed over a period of time spent roughly equal amounts of time in collaborative learning about processes and content. There was less attention to "people processes" than to technical or administrative processes, but it was clear that fifteen years of experience with their quality programs had taught them the importance of process learning.

In other well-known companies we also see differing preferences. Among those who have invested heavily in process learning are Federal Express, American Airlines, Citibank, and Westpak (an Australian bank). These organizations were early learners about how to use information technology to improve the processes through which they deliver their product. They developed "software factories" that have functioned as veritable learning laboratories. For example, Citibank developed a leading low-cost credit card business out of this investment. In a more limited application, Williams Company, a leading builder and operator of oil and gas pipelines, applied process knowledge to the use of pipelines for fiber optic networks. Special mention should be made of Neiman-Marcus, which seems to have developed equally impressive learning about content and process. Its stores epitomize a combination of top-flight deliverables supported by great concern for process.

Knowledge Reserve

This Learning Orientation refers to variations in behaviors and attitudes as to the repositories of knowledge. At one pole, knowledge is seen in very personal terms as something an individual possesses by virtue of education and experience. This is the kind of knowledge lost when an old hand leaves an organization; processes and insights evaporate because they were not made a part of a collective memory. This approach legitimizes highly subjective ways of knowing. At the other pole, the emphasis is on defining knowledge in more objective, social terms, as being a consensually supported result of information processing. It emphasizes organizational memory or a publicly documented body of known things. The difference in these approaches is between "manualized" know-how and an individual craftsman's knowledge.

Nonaka (1991), borrowing from M. Polyani's distinction between tacit and explicit knowledge, has shown how both of these approaches exist in a dynamic relationship in a knowledge-creating setting. He shows how an organization can move from one to the other in order to leverage organizational learning. In a highly provocative paper, Brown and Duguid (1991) show how Xerox service representatives use their personal, undocumented knowledge to solve problems beyond the letter of their manuals. Despite the obvious utility of both modes, we find differences in organizational preference. Much of the difference seems to be based on cultural assumptions about what knowledge is usable. In some settings, personal knowledge is seen as subjective; in others it is valued as informed intuition. Explicit, shared knowledge is often valued as objective, yet in other settings it is seen as generalizations that do not fit any single actual case.

The Investment Funds Group of MIC makes available to its analysts and fund managers a great deal of information about companies and investment opportunities, but there are no policy statements or operating procedure manuals on how to use it. In keeping with its corporate culture, which values individualism, the environment makes it possible for individuals to learn a great deal, but there is little pressure to codify the learning. Although engaged in a business that values hard data, the group supports subjective, tacit knowledge in decision-making processes.

At Fiat Auto's technical division the individual has historically been the repository of knowledge. This continues to be true but is being augmented by efforts to establish a *memoria technica,* or engineering knowledge bank. EDF prefers a collective, explicit Knowledge Reserve, using its performance feedback system to create a shared repository of lessons learned from successful operation and from system or component failures. Motorola shows evidence of both but works hard to make knowledge explicit and available on a broad basis. Much effort is spent at many levels to document experience and to codify it in ways that demystify.

Preferences are also seen in other well-known organizations. Financial service firms, law firms, and the publishing and motion picture industries tend to have a strong preference for seeing knowledge in personal terms. This may be due to strong values about individual creativity and to loose forms of organization. However, most religious, military, and government organizations invest heavily in public, explicit documentation.

Dissemination Mode

Although related to Knowledge Reserve, this Learning Orientation pertains to differences between establishing an atmosphere in which learning evolves informally and one in which a more structured, controlled approach is taken to induce learning. In the formal approach, a decision is made that a valuable insight or method should be shared and used by others on a broad, institutionalized basis. Various forms of written communication and formal educational methods are generally employed for this purpose. Another way to disseminate learning is through written procedures.

In the informal approach, learning is spread through encounters with role models and gatekeepers who actualize the insight or method by behaving in a compelling way. Another version of the informal approach is the kind of learning that occurs when members of an occupational group or work team share their experiences in ongoing dialogue. We can think of this as learning through a process of osmosis. It assumes that learning will be shared if the learners have an opportunity to mingle with each other. It further assumes that learning cannot always be managed or controlled, and that it may be inhibited by efforts to do so. Lave and Wenger (1991) referred to this as learning through "communities of practice" and suggest that it will take place as a result of the social nature of most work. Charles Lindbloom (Lindbloom and Cohen, 1979) has written eloquently on how usable knowledge is both generated and shared in a social setting. Organizational policies and rules can act to enhance this learning or they can act as barriers to its fulfillment. In this vein, it is interesting to see the recent proliferation of formal and informal networks in many organizations. This movement is an attempt to develop vehicles for sharing of knowledge in complex, fast-moving, and loosely coupled work groups.

The Investment Funds Group of MIC clearly prefers an informal Dissemination Mode in which learning develops and is shared in loosely organized interactions. Motorola shows evidence of supporting both approaches, although it invests heavily in structured, firmwide programs when it comes to a basic value or method that senior management wants institutionalized. Motorola University appears to have been created partly for this reason. The area of quality was considered so critical that the dissemination effort now includes vendors and customers. Recently, vendors in certain areas were told that they had to compete for the Baldrige Award in order to be on the company's approved vendor list.

EDF prefers formal modes, emphasizing documented procedures that are available to all. Fiat Auto's Direzione Technica disseminates knowledge in a formal process whereby it is accumulated in specialist departments and then shared through staff participation in cross-functional design teams. Interestingly, Fiat expects that more informal dissemination will occur as these teams have more experience together.

Examples of use of informal modes in other sites include several research-oriented universities, such as MIT, and many investment banking firms. Mandated approaches are also seen in Arthur Andersen Consulting, where younger members are exposed to highly standardized learning experiences. Andersen created its large training campus and educational center in St. Charles, Illinois, to assist in this endeavor. Disney appears to follow this mode in training people to work in its theme parks, yet it supports more informal modes in the divisions that design new products.

Learning Scope

This Learning Orientation pertains to whether knowledge is focused on methods and tools to improve what is already known or being done, or on knowledge that challenges the assumptions about what is known or done. The difference is whether learning is directed at the enhancement of existing paradigms, products, or services, or toward creating new ones. Argyris and Schön (1978) refer to the former as single-loop learning and the latter as double-loop learning. They argue that organizational performance problems are more likely to require a change in prevalent assumptions than improvement in existing modes. The difference is between an efficiency exercise and an experimental approach, between incremental learning and transformative learning. An example is whether a firm invests in improving the efficiency of an assembly line or in studies to find alternatives to the assembly line.

In recent years organizational learning theorists have focused on the transformative side, arguing that incremental learning is not sufficient to solve the complex problems facing organizations. However, we see these learning capabilities as complementing, not competing against, each other. If an organization is constantly transforming itself it will never settle into predictable, stable performance levels. Incrementalism serves as a reinforcer of learning; it is the way skills are honed and polished. Of course, if the learning investments are all directed toward improving present conditions, the organization limits its ability to envision a possibly better future. Thus the need is to use the approach required at a given time and invest in it. Organizations may have a preference for one mode over the other, but a sound learning system can benefit from learning using both approaches.

The organizations we studied display a range of behavior in this regard. Nuclear Power Operations at EDF is primarily focused on incremental learning and does little questioning of basic assumptions. It prides itself on being the world's major nuclear power utility and devotes significant resources to the task of being the safest and most efficient operator through small improvements rather than transformations. Fiat Auto's engineering division is becoming more balanced. Its traditional engineering groups' learning is corrective and incremental, but in its new cross-functional teams there is support for innovative thinking and new product development. Motorola appears to be well balanced in its orientation. Acceptance by the founding family of the concept of "organizational renewal" has led to far-reaching and courageous changes in the company's product lines through the years.

Once a new direction is chosen, the dedication to efficient learning is powerful. The Investment Funds Group of MIC shows a pattern that is slightly more adaptive than innovative. There is constant attention to corrective action concerning investment decisions, but the group can engage in examination of its assumptions when confronted with disconfirming feedback.

Interesting examples of firms that have recently invested heavily in transformative learning are Semco (Semler, 1993, 1994) and Oticon (Kolind, 1994; LaBarre, 1994). Semco, a well-established, diverse Brazilian firm, embarked on a transformation about fifteen years ago and has questioned just about every assumption underlying the way it did business. A program of ongoing experimentation was entered into, resulting in evolving structural and process changes. For example, at present Semco has no central information system, involves employees in developing wage and salaries systems (of which there were several in 1994), and has very loose job descriptions and work hours.

Oticon decided to change itself from a manufacturer of hearing aids to a knowledge-based firm specializing in all kinds of auditory problems, such as those of concert halls and other public places. In the process it experimented with major changes in organization and work-layout design, including providing employees with workstations at home, and a program in which all employees work on at least one project of their own choosing.

The point is not that these two firms developed unusual ways of doing business but that they invested in learning that challenged their old assumptions.

Value-Chain Focus

This Learning Orientation indicates which core competences and learning investments are valued and supported. It reflects an assumption that the organization can gain a competitive advantage through its ability to add value at a particular point in the value chain that other firms cannot. Although it is nice to think that all steps in the value chain are important, there are limits to the number of areas in which firms can develop competence; thus choices are made to focus on some at the expense of others. It follows, whether or not it is explicitly stated, that more resources will be devoted to the achievement of excellence in the chosen areas. When a firm is notably engineering-focused or marketing-driven, it is safe to assume that it is biased in favor of substantial learning investments in that area over time. It then stands to reason that more robust learning will have occurred in that area. Prahalad and Hamel, in their seminal paper (1990) on core competences, observe that a decision to exit a function or stage in the value chain and to have an alliance with another firm that performs that service amounts to a decision to "de-invest" in ongoing learning in that area.

In defining the value chain for present purposes, we have taken some liberties and divided it into two categories: activities of an internally directed "design-and-make" nature and those of a more externally focused "market-and-deliver" nature. The former category includes R&D, engineering, and manufacturing. The latter includes sales, distribution, and service activities. We recognize that this does some disservice to the value-chain concept, but it easily accounts for most of what we observed. In addition, we believe the design-and-make and market-and-deliver categories apply equally well to service- and product-oriented groups.

At the Investment Funds Group of MIC the focus is clearly on the design-and-make side and on the nature of the products. This is balanced by learning investments on the market-and-deliver side among its marketing staff, but there is a strong boundary between these groups and the fund management side is regarded as the core of the organization. Motorola's total quality effort clearly recognizes the importance of both sides of the value-added chain, but the design-and-make side is significantly ahead of the market-and-deliver side in learning investments around quality. Fiat Auto's engineering division is clearly oriented toward the design-and-make side, though its new system of simultaneous engineering is forcing it toward increased sensitivity to the other side as well. EDF's Nuclear Power Operations focuses squarely on efficient production.

Among other well-known firms, Digital Equipment Corporation's learning investments traditionally were much more heavily focused on the design-and-make side. Procter & Gamble has a long history of investing in market-and-deliver as well as in design-and-make. Under Harold Geneen ITT took a different path by investing heavily in financial aspects and forcing its managers to be competent in this area. GM's Saturn Motor Division is a highly interesting case in that its founding assumption was that it would be an innovator on both ends of the value chain. Seeing Saturn's success, we can assume that learning investments of some magnitude were made in each area.

Learning Focus

This distinction is between learning geared to individual skill development and learning focused on team or group skill development. Team or group learning has received much attention in recent literature on organizational learning (Marsick, Dechant, and Kasl, 1991; Senge, 1990). These authors have argued that collaborative learning is better for organizational purposes than individual learning and that team skills such as coordination, decision making, and so forth are sorely needed in today's interdependent, networked world. Others have shown how U.S. product development and production has been hampered by lack of cooperation among interdependent groups (Dertouzos, Lester, and Solow, 1989).

We totally support the need for team skills but believe that both individual and group skill development are necessary and that it might help to look at them as stylistic choices rather than seeing them in normative terms. Even Peter Senge (1990)—a strong proponent of team learning—makes a plea for enhancement of "personal mastery," which is essentially individual learning. We think it is important for organizations to assess how they are doing in both areas and take action for improvement in either one. It is useful to develop better ways of integrating individual learning programs with group development.

The Investment Funds Group of MIC promotes individual learning, which fits with its individualistic culture and its individual reward system. It is not at all clear to us that heavy investment in team learning would improve the effectiveness of the group, which is really an aggregation of individual investment experts. Perhaps analysts and fund managers might do better as a team, but this is difficult to accomplish without changing the reward system to an overall group performance incentive. However, MIC's marketing groups are more supportive of collective learning and are now investing in team development as one way to improve their effectiveness as a total unit.

Fiat Auto's engineering division has been more oriented toward individual development. However, with its new reliance on cross-functional work teams, group development is increasingly more important. Motorola has become more team-oriented in recent years and is making heavier investments in collaborative learning. The Motorola executive groups observed by us were consciously designed to foster collective learning about two strategic issues affecting the entire company. Although this intervention clearly promoted better understanding among people with different backgrounds, much more effort was devoted to the content of the problem than to teaching skills that would enable them to work well as a team. As Motorola is using more and more teams, documented cases of team development in the firm have now appeared (Katzenback and Smith, 1993).

At EDF both individual and group development are employed, especially with respect to control room teams. All EDF employees follow individual training programs to be certified in their craft or to prepare them for promotion. Control room teams also learn together, in groups, through the use of plant simulators.

Examples of other firms with emphasis on team learning are Federal Express, with its heavy investment in teams for its quality effort, and Herman Miller, with its long-term emphasis on participative management and the Scanlon Plan.

The Role of Learning Orientations in Building Learning Capability

The seven Learning Orientations represent the critical dimensions in describing or characterizing how organizational learning takes place. In effect, LOrs provide a focal point for depicting the learning capability in all organizations. In an ideal world, firms would make learning investments in all aspects of their business and would be good at the fourteen approaches represented by the seven LOrs.

However, we find few that are able to do this. An imbalance may reflect, for example, the vision of the founders of an enterprise such that the effort to launch the business is so highly focused in a certain area that other aspects are given less attention. In other cases, experience over time shows that some things work better than others in producing an effective organization. A preference emerges, greater investment is made in what works, and a value becomes institutionalized. For whatever reasons, more is learned in some places or functions within the firm than in others.

A similar pattern develops as to how learning is to be accomplished. Is it to be accomplished by creating a supportive environment in which learning emerges by letting competent people "do their thing"? By identifying important skills and attitudes and then educating large numbers of employees in these through programmatic means? Or through apprenticeships in which learners work closely with models from whom they can learn? The ideal organization will support all these, yet we find significant differences among organizations as to their preferences and support of these different modes.

Once attitudes or values about what to learn and how to learn are established, they become absorbed in the everyday life of the organization. They become powerful processes that guide managerial behavior. The orientations can function as choices made in full awareness or become covert drivers of decisions and serve as unquestioned assumptions. In either case, without making these values explicit and examining them carefully, it is not likely that significant changes will occur. Once the assumptions and their consequences are understood fully, a choice can be made to accept these values and build on them or to look at and build on other assumptions.

Together, the seven Learning Orientations form a picture of the existent learning processes in any organization. We did not formulate the LOrs as criteria to evaluate an organization's learning capability but as characteristics that help us understand and describe that capability. For this reason, they comprise that section of our overall framework that is consistent with the capability perspective. LOrs remind us about the transparency of learning, which comes in many forms. The next chapter discusses the normative or evaluative side of our framework: the Facilitating Factors.

Case Study:
Nuclear Power Operations at Electricité de France

Electricité de France (EDF) is the world's leading producer of electricity from nuclear fuel. Presently EDF operates fifty-six nuclear power plants that generate approximately 75 percent of France's electricity. EDF's system of nuclear power generation is built on the premise that by having many plants of the same basic design, knowledge of how these machines work efficiently and safely can easily be accumulated over time. This knowledge can identify and solve generic problems so that uncertainties in running nuclear plants can be reduced.

How Learning Occurs

Nuclear power plants are designed on the basis of known technical and regulated systems, so periodic inspections can be made on various system components through measuring or calibrating tangible characteristics. Machines that must perform under certain atmospheric conditions—temperature, pressure, humidity, stress, or the like—can be tested or monitored by measuring the factors that affect performance. For example, the thickness of a pipe weld can be measured to ascertain the probability that leakage will occur. Such tests and equipment calibrations generate knowledge of actual operating conditions that can be compared with design or regulated conditions. When there is a difference, that knowledge or information can be disseminated and action taken to rectify the situation. Corrective action alters the probability that unforeseen and unwanted events will occur, thereby improving safety and reducing the risk of an unplanned shutdown.

The process of creating, disseminating, and utilizing knowledge about performance to improve or increase the efficiency of nuclear plants is referred to at EDF as the *retour d'expérience*. It is possible to look at how performance feedback can be used to increase the efficiency of a given nuclear power plant, but EDF as an organizational system is designed to enhance the sharing and application of information that comes from the performance of many plants. EDF has created structures and processes designed to serve this feedback system. Through lessons learned from past problems, EDF personnel are able to identify defects or limitations in the design, construction, or maintenance of equipment. Preprogrammed steps are then followed to maintain systems or create conditions that lower the risk of system failure. In effect, through operational experience EDF builds its repertoire of preventive maintenance to reduce problems or defects that lead to system failure. Operational experience may also lead to redesign or system modifications.

The nature of nuclear power plant technology and the design and culture of EDF as a network of similar, interconnected plants creates an organizational environment that establishes certain preconditions for learning. For example, staff are expected to act on the basis of recognizing the interdependencies between plants and how the experience of one plant may be a barometer for others. One challenge is determining whether a particular defect is unique to the plant where the problem occurred or is a generic problem that should be of concern to similar plants. The types of interventions and processes used to explore and address generic versus idiosyncratic problems are quite distinct. Understanding and solving generic problems or defects involves a greater number of interorganizational and intergroup exchanges than problems that can be easily and appropriately addressed at a given plant.

When events occur at nuclear power plants worldwide, they are reported to the Paris headquarters of Exploitation du Parc Nucléaire (EPN). For those that occur at EDF plants, site staff complete a *fiche événement* or *fiche d'analomie de matériel* within forty-eight hours of the event. Site staff then have two months to complete a primary-level analysis. At EPN headquarters, events (both internal and external to EDF operations) that took place the previous week are reviewed weekly at a Friday morning interdepartmental meeting facilitated by the Groupe Animation Retour d'Expérience.

The following Monday afternoon another, larger interdepartmental meeting is convened to review the events listed as meriting further analysis as actual or potential generic problems or defects and to follow-up studies and analyses in progress. This meeting is convened by the Groupe Coordination du Parc. Special studies are commissioned as needed to research defects on a long-term basis. Such studies usually involve multiple divisions at EDF and contracted personnel. EPN pilots work committees (*groupes de travail*) to review on an ongoing basis the progress of such studies.

It may take one to two years to complete all relevant research and present a course of action. Study groups may recommend permanent modifications that can take an additional five years to be implemented at all pertinent sites. After the second-level analysis has been completed, a *groupe des experts* may be formed to review recommendations and decide on their implementation.

EDF's Learning Orientations

EDF's Knowledge Source is mainly internal, but there is some valuing of external knowledge; it does learn from events that take place at foreign plants. The engineering focus in Nuclear Power Operations emphasizes a process rather than product approach and a design-and-make function rather than a marketing function. Knowledge Reserve is public; EDF's performance feedback system creates a shared repository of lessons learned from system and component failures. Regulatory requirements demand procedural ways of working; consequently, Dissemination Mode is highly formal. Learning Scope is clearly oriented toward the incremental. EDF emphasizes individual learning, but attention is also given to group training, especially through the use of simulators to train control room teams. EDF's focus on making incremental changes to the design of its plants based on its own operating experience reflects a learning style emphasizing correction using internal knowledge. When EDF generates knowledge through the analysis of a critical incident, the result is often a change in bureaucratic procedure. This dissemination approach ensures that everyone has access to the proper way to perform so that the recurrence of accidents can be avoided.

4

Why Organizations Learn
Facilitating Factors

The second section of our integrated model of organizational learning capability consists of Facilitating Factors (FFs) that promote learning in any setting. Unlike Learning Orientations, which are descriptive of generic learning approaches that are neither good nor bad, Facilitating Factors are normative. That is, the more each is prevalent in an organizational unit the more opportunity exists for learning. The ease and amount of learning depends on the strength of these factors. Collectively, they determine an organization's learning potential. This chapter covers the ten Facilitating Factors in our framework and includes, at the end, a brief description of why learning occurs at another of the sites we studied in depth—the Investment Funds Group at MIC.

Best Practices to Enhance Organizational Learning

Facilitating Factors are the practices or conditions that promote learning within all kinds of organizations. We derived them from looking at critical incidents of learning at a number of organizations and then applied them to an assessment of other organizational settings. The presence of these factors determines the efficiency and effectiveness of the organizational learning cycle. We see them as establishing an organization's learning potential; they do not guarantee that useful learning will occur, but if they are lacking, it is almost certain that the ability of the organization to adapt to its environment or to engage in generative learning will be severely hampered. In a sense, they are like catalysts or lubricants that determine how well an engine performs.

This section of our model embraces the normative perspective discussed in Chapter One and comes close to defining the "learning organization" as Senge and others have defined it. The ten FFs described here overlap and extend Senge's five disciplines as well as those of other modelers such as Garvin. They provide the necessary and sufficient conditions that allow learning to emerge and flourish. The organizational units we studied varied in the extent to which the factors were prevalent, and some units that were very good in certain factors were deemed only marginally effective in others. None were seen as highly competent in all ten factors. However, in aggregate the factors explain why organizational learning occurs. Indeed, when applied to approximately fifty organizational units the power of the ten factors as a group was evident.

Each factor is summarized in the following list and discussed separately afterward. The sequence of presentation is based on the portion of the organizational learning cycle each factor influences the most.

1. *Scanning Imperative.* People gather information about conditions and practices outside their own unit; they seek out information about the external environment.

2. *Performance Gap.* Shared perception of a gap between current and desired performance.

3. *Concern for Measurement.* Considerable effort is spent defining and measuring key factors. Discourse over metrics is regarded as a learning activity.

4. *Organizational Curiosity.* Curiosity about conditions and practices, interest in creative ideas and new technologies, support for experimentation.

5. *Climate of Openness.* Organizational members communicate openly; problems, errors, or lessons are shared, not hidden.

6. *Continuous Education.* The organization is committed to providing high-quality resources for learning.

7. *Operational Variety.* Members value different methods, procedures, and competences; they appreciate diversity.

8. *Multiple Advocates.* New ideas and methods can be advanced by employees at all organizational levels. Multiple advocates or champions exist.

9. *Involved Leadership.* Leaders are personally and actively involved in learning initiatives and in ensuring that a learning environment is maintained.

10. *Systems Perspective.* Recognition of interdependence among organizational units and groups; awareness of time delay between actions and their outcomes.

Scanning Imperative

This Facilitating Factor pertains to an ongoing effort to scan the environment for information. Sound learning cannot occur without a foundation of enhanced consciousness or a thorough understanding of one's environment. Scanning Imperative is a basic process for increasing awareness that can lead to learning. An organization that does not value what is "out there" and does not have a well-assimilated acceptance of the importance of eternal vigilance limits the range and depth of its knowledge. To engage in scanning does not imply that an organization will simply borrow from or adapt what others are doing. Scanning is a way of sensing developing problems or opportunities and acting on them early rather than waiting until a problem is full-blown or a window of opportunity has closed. Scanning is an organization's scouting function; it provides the stimulation and direction of knowledge generation.

Much has been written in recent years about the importance of environmental scanning, especially with regard to market opportunities. There is substantial agreement that many firms get themselves into trouble because of limited or poorly directed efforts in this regard. This shortcoming contributes to marketing myopia. In response, many firms have gone to great lengths to increase their scanning capacity, though some did so only when they finally realized that internal information and skills were insufficient to solve a problem or avoid a crisis. For example, Motorola found that five years of work to improve quality using just its own internal knowledge resulted in only modest improvements. A significant scanning effort in which Motorola's operating executives studied first-hand what others, particularly Japanese companies, were doing resulted in substantial changes and the achievement of the first Baldrige Award four years later. By contrast, it seems fair to say that mainframe computer manufacturers (Cray, Unisys, IBM) ran into difficulties when they failed to sense developing trends early enough. The same may be said of U.S. automobile companies in the 1970s, who are only now regaining their competitive edge after better attention to environmental scanning. Other organizational units and firms have turned a desire to get closer to their customer into a Scanning Imperative.

It is hard to disagree with the imperative to improve scanning, but the task of developing and implementing an appropriate strategy for it is not an easy one. There are many questions to be answered: Who should be responsible for doing it, all the members of a unit or a small number of "scanning specialists"? What kind of information will be useful? Should there be a focus on broad social and economic trends, competitors' strategies and actions, customer needs, or all these? And finally, what is the implication for units within a firm that deliver products and services to others within the firm? What is the nature of effective scanning for these groups? Do they look only at their internal customers or do they study how similar groups work in other firms? There are no easy answers to these questions, but one indicator of organizational learning potential is the extent to which managers deploy resources in scanning activities. For example, companies that allocate travel funds for staff to attend business conferences and expos increase their chances of learning.

Performance Gap

Performance Gap is the shared awareness of organizational members that there is a difference between the organization's desired performance and actual performance. There are two aspects to this FF.

The first aspect has to do with the kind of analysis managers use to reveal a Performance Gap. When feedback shows a gap between desired and actual performance, managers respond with actions they hope will correct the problem. But three kinds of problems often act as barriers to recognizing or responding to a Performance Gap:

1. Use of the wrong kinds of measures to identify critical performance factors (for example, using financial accounting measures where operating or nonfinancial indicators might be more useful). A good discussion of this issue is found in the work of Kaplan and Norton (1992) on the "balanced scorecard."

2. Lack of a Systems Perspective from which the problem must be studied. This is discussed in greater detail later where we deal with Systems Perspective as a critical Facilitating Factor in its own right.

3. A long period (sometimes many years) of positive performance results. This causes people to become complacent and resistant to critical self-examination. It also leads to easy rationalizations or "theories of exceptional happenings" when negative, possibly disconfirming, feedback is perceived.

When staff are inhibited by these barriers, learning from experience is diminished. The potential for learning is proportional to how widely performance gap concerns are shared. In our studies, one of the best instances of how perception of Performance Gap can lead to adaptive learning can be found at the Nuclear Power Operations of Electricité de France. Supported by the nature of the nuclear power business, variations in performance become the catalyst for a learning effort to reachieve the prescribed standard. Any disconfirming feedback is shared throughout the network of operating power plants, and study teams go to work to see what they can learn not only about how to deal with a single incident but about how to change things on a broader basis.

The second aspect of this factor has to do with a growing awareness of achieving higher performance or of a way of being more effective than envisioned before. There is a vision of new outcomes that are not simply incremental extensions of prior goals, a vision that suggests a qualitatively new way of seeing or doing something. An example of a new vision is organizing work through horizontal networks as opposed to functional "smokestacks," or envisioning what it would take to have a totally defect-free production line as opposed to one in which there are incremental improvements over time and an acceptance of the inevitability of having some defects.

Awareness of a Performance Gap—either through analysis of performance shortfalls or a new vision—opens the door to learning by providing the initial awareness that new knowledge needs to be generated or that something needs to be "unlearned." As a consequence of its 1984 benchmarking studies of total quality in other firms, this recognition became very apparent to Motorola executives and produced intense forces for new learning. Several years ago this same recognition hit Fiat Auto's engineering division and sparked interest in learning how to be more effective in new product development. Motorola and MIC have benefited for some years by having highly future-oriented CEOs who acted as catalysts for formulation of new visions.

As with Scanning Imperative, improving an organization's ability to learn as a result of Performance Gap is not a simple matter.

Asking anyone to face up to and accept feedback or to accept a vision that means giving up a deeply held world view is to challenge the very core of an individual's professional and personal identity. There is no way to accomplish this change simply by logic and analytical reasoning. Anyone who doubts the difficulty of this task is referred to the well-documented case of the space shuttle *Challenger*. A disaster resulted because of failure to achieve a shared perception of emerging but disconfirming feedback. Attempts to reason logically only served to rationalize deep-seated concerns.

Concern for Measurement

All managers measure performance one way or another and in doing so accept the general measurement practices that are customary in their function, company, or industry. As part of feedback systems, measures help managers decide whether they are on course or if corrections are needed. In this sense, measurement is part of any adaptive learning system. In our studies and in the work of others another aspect of this concern became apparent. This has to do with the way managers in some organizations view measurement as part of a learning process rather than as purely for monitoring and control. In these instances we noted that managers, even at senior levels, discuss the need for metrics that will give them new and different information than they have been accustomed to. This discussion includes such issues as the balance between internally focused data gathering and information external to the unit (such as customer attitudes toward quality and service). Moreover, it focuses on the development of measures by the people involved and on customized as well as standard measures. In short, extended consideration of measurement issues becomes a critical part of learning. It affords a concrete way of getting all participants' mental models out in the open.

The importance of metrics in total quality management (TQM) programs has been well documented (for example, see Schmidt and Finnigan, 1992). Many organizations claim that the development of their own metrics and measurement programs made a huge difference in the success of TQM. Motorola executives believe that Concern for Measurement and the development of their own metric systems were important reasons for the success of their program. As a result of this discovery, senior executives at Motorola now spend a great deal of their time examining and developing metrics for strategic initiatives, often developing their own measurement programs rather than delegating this to staff specialists.

Because measurement is an ongoing management activity, one for which a skill base and a body of knowledge already exists to some degree, this factor may be easier to enhance than some of the other Facilitating Factors. Managers do not need to be convinced of the importance of measurement; they need to be motivated to see the value of approaching a problem with an open mind concerning what needs to be measured and how their involvement in metric development provides a powerful learning experience.

Organizational Curiosity

This factor refers to support for trying new things, curiosity about how things work, and the ability to "play around" with policies, methods, and procedures. Organizational Curiosity fosters an environment in which people are encouraged to try out things on an ongoing basis. If we believe that experience creates learning, it follows that engaging in more kinds of experiences will lead to more learning. Unless the structuring of work at all stages of the value chain is seen as today's experiment or experience gathering, as opposed to "the best way," learning will be retarded. In effect, any organization that wants to improve its learning capabilities needs many people who think and act like applied research scientists or children at play while they are delivering goods and services. This point of view is supported by Dorothy Leonard-Barton (1992), who considers the next production frontier to be the organization of the factory as a learning laboratory. The concept of continuous improvement derives from similar reasoning; it assumes that the way things are done today may not be the way they are done tomorrow.

Organizational Curiosity cannot be developed and maintained if people are punished when they try something new and it fails or is less effective than the old way. Sitkin (1992) has written eloquently on the importance of "small failures" in promoting organizational learning. Intellectually this is seen as sound reasoning, yet many organizations are reluctant to engage in anything called an experiment or a pilot. Using other terms, such as "new way," to describe experiments might help ease this reluctance. A few organizations deal with this problem by creating parallel systems in which new ways are tried out while the old is kept in place to minimize disruption and as insurance. Obviously this cannot be attempted without making resources available to both approaches. Thus, without some degree of slack, learning is inhibited. As most organizations are reluctant to tamper with predictability, the best way to develop Organizational Curiosity may be to adopt a plan for small, evolutionary experiments rather than to contemplate revolutionary tryouts.

We observed few instances where Organizational Curiosity was strong. One of these seemed to be Motorola's Paging Products Operation, where we observed the current production line for one product, the blueprint and preparation for a new setup to replace the current line, and a "white room" laboratory in which research was under way for the line that would later replace the one just being installed. This comes close to what Leonard-Barton has in mind when she talks about the factory as a learning laboratory. MIC also seems to tinker constantly with its product offerings and delivery systems. Among companies known to act on the basis of Organizational Curiosity, we note WalMart and 3M. At WalMart, on any given day there are about 250 experiments being conducted. These are concentrated in the areas of sales promotion, product display, and customer service. Although 3M is in many ways a traditional firm, staff attitudes toward new product development and operational unit size are indicative of Organizational Curiosity. Many entrepreneurial ventures show a similar trait in the early stages of their development.

Climate of Openness

This factor is related to the permeability of information boundaries and the degree to which opportunities to observe and to participate are available to organization members. If an organizational unit is interested in enhancing its learning capabilities, it must examine the extent to which it has open boundaries. When there are tight controls over information or rigid rules about who belongs at planning and problem-solving meetings, only the fortunate few who are allowed to participate in the largest number and variety of events are provided with rich learning opportunities. Lave and Wenger (1991) have espoused the notion of "legitimate peripheral participation" as a guideline for examining this. Openness is also a characteristic of open-book management.

This issue cannot be dealt with only through formal structures; much learning is a function of daily, unplanned interactions among people. In addition to letting employees watch peers and higher levels of management at work, informal contacts allow people to pursue interesting relationships on their own. Among the best examples of a strong Climate of Openness we know of are the Oticon and Semco cases referred to in Chapter Three. In these situations there are few barriers to communication or information sharing. Likewise, in a thousand-person environmental consulting firm with which we consult there are more than thirty formal and informal networks that enhance communication and participation.

This factor also includes the freedom with which people can express their views and the permissible degree of disagreement and debate. If the organizational climate is such that a high degree of politeness and conformity are rewarded, many potentially important views will not be made available. Related to this is the extent to which mistakes are shared and not hidden. Argyris (1985) has made a cogent argument that organizational learning is severely hampered by managers' widespread habit of acting defensively, of covering up or hiding errors to avoid punishment.

Improving Climate of Openness is difficult; deeply entrenched assumptions about trust and control are strong barriers. In some cases improvement requires a leap of faith that can only succeed if supported by the actions of senior leaders who model openness and trust and do not punish staff who share information about problems or errors. A recent study by the MIT Center for Organizational Learning at a major automobile company found that great success was achieved in getting people involved in a new car development project to increase the number of problems that were openly reported, as against the usual practice of hiding them or passing them on to others later in the chain. Although this resulted in huge cost savings and significant shortening of the time to market, those in charge of the project were required to defend the number and early occurrence of problems, and their credibility became suspect. Some time after the project was completed, the leader was removed from his job. So much for openness!

Continuous Education

By Continuous Education we mean the internalization of a commitment to lifelong education at all levels of the organization. To constantly develop organizational learning capability is to engage in an ongoing, never-ending process. It is all but impossible to accept the notion of knowledge as a competitive weapon without realizing that learning does not end. Peter Senge's discipline of "personal mastery" is another way of looking at this factor, as is the Samurai tradition of masters never ceasing to practice and learn. Another indicator of this factor is the extent to which these values permeate the entire organization, not just the training and development function. The achievement of a high level of Continuous Education requires work settings that support learning of all kinds, ranging from on-the-job and apprenticeship experiences to company-supported individual initiatives to seek out knowledge and improve skills.

The development of enhanced capability in Continuous Education cannot be accomplished without a significant, ongoing commitment of resources. Organizations on the leading edge devote to education of all kinds a percentage of their annual budget roughly equivalent to that devoted to research and development or advertising and promotion. They invest heavily in formal education programs but reach further to a more pervasive support of all kinds of developmental experiences. Merely to have courses for employees is not enough to merit a high score for Continuous Education. Many organizations fool themselves into thinking that they are adequate because they have a catalog of courses or operate an internal "university." This is a necessary but not sufficient condition that calls for acquiring a palpable sense that there are many kinds of learning experiences. Moreover, this holds for all levels of the organization from the CEO to the lowest-level employee.

Of the organizations we studied intensively, MIC and Motorola stand out in this regard. MIC's chairman is known as a seeker of knowledge in many areas, not just financial matters. Although most of the effort at MIC focuses on powerful learning experiences for younger professional employees, the firm makes it possible for fund managers and analysts to access all kinds of information and knowledge that are considered important. In keeping with the individualistic culture of this firm, people are expected to take a great deal of responsibility for their own learning.

Motorola has vigorously embraced the concept of Continuous Education. It has a policy that every employee must receive some formal educational experience each year and has assigned on-the-job and classroom experiences for all levels of management, including senior executives. In 1992 Motorola spent 3.6 percent of its revenues on education, including contracts with community colleges for employee education. Among its programs is one in which fifteen to twenty upper-middle-level managers spend one year in part-time study of a topic of their choosing and present the result to the board of directors.

Among firms not studied intensively by us, we can point to General Electric, Unilever, and Royal Dutch Shell as having valued Continuous Education at all levels for many years. Unilever and Shell provide developmental assignments that enable managers to gain work experience in many parts of the world. In this way, they help managers acquire an international perspective and use their skill base.

From a strategic point of view, the first thing to realize is that no organization can possibly do everything by relying only on its own planning and resources. To enhance capability in this area also requires a setting in which individuals are encouraged to arrange their own learning experiences. To build learning capability, organization leaders must provide schemes in which people select their developmental experiences, search out learning opportunities within and without the company, and take personal responsibility in general for their own continuous learning.

Operational Variety

This factor is a companion to Organizational Curiosity in that it implies that there is more than one way to accomplish work goals. It assumes that an organization that supports variation in strategy, policy, process, structure, and personnel is more adaptable when unforeseen problems arise. It provides more options and, perhaps even more important, allows for the development of multiple role models. If an organization manifests several ways of doing something or has flexible work rules, its members can see different means to an end. This pluralism helps to enhance learning in a way that an absolutist approach does not. Operational Variety is an extremely important factor in organizational learning capability because it provides an opportunity to understand the implications and consequences of different ways of working. In fact, we see Operational Variety as a kind of litmus test of an organization's readiness to learn.

From the standpoint of traditional organizational concepts of predictability and efficiency, Operational Variety is an annoyance.

It is much harder to discipline and control staff when they value multiple approaches or flexible interpretation of rules and variations of "best practice." Since the development of scientific management early in this century, managers have been rewarded for maintaining stability and consistency in their operations. In this sense, as with some of our other factors, the call for a more hospitable learning environment can raise fears that efficiency will decline seriously. Some organizations have balanced these seemingly disparate objectives by setting up new operations to try an alternate way without giving up a customary way of doing business ("greenfield sites"). The creation of Saturn by General Motors is an example of how Operational Variety can be developed within an existing corporation.

We did not see a great deal of variety at sites we studied intensively. An exception is MIC's Fixed Income Group, where we identified at least three different methods or systems used by fund managers in making investment decisions. Senior management, although a bit skeptical about one approach, was willing to support all three as legitimate. This was supported by a bottom-line orientation that placed more emphasis on results than on how they were obtained. An example of Operational Variety in a case reported by others is found at Semco, discussed earlier. Semco has a number of different compensation systems; employees can elect the one they prefer. For example, they can work on straight salary, on an incentive basis, as independent contractors, or they can set up their own business and sell their services to Semco. Most managers would throw up their hands in exasperation at this multiplicity, but it seems to work well at Semco and is seen as a strong contributor to the company's learning atmosphere.

Multiple Advocates

Although Involved Leadership (discussed after this) is a prerequisite for enhancing the acquisition, dissemination, and utilization of knowledge, in order for knowledge to be effectively utilized Multiple Advocates are essential. We found that unless a significant number of people act as champions, a developing base of knowledge does not become broadly used. When acting alone, change or learning advocates can too easily be dismissed as deviants or malcontents. The greater the number of advocates who promote a new idea and the greater the number of "gatekeepers" who bring knowledge into the system, the more rapidly and extensively will true organizational learning take place.

To make any skill or piece of knowledge useful to many members of the organization, a number of respected, key members of the organization must be seen as using it and trying to influence others regarding its value. Advocates serve several purposes. In addition to being "preachers," they serve as role models for others to observe. This supports generalization of the learning to new situations. Also, the more people who promote a learning mode, the more learning in general is encouraged.

Two significant change efforts that we studied failed largely because the CEOs were the only visible champions for learning. Although knowledge was acquired and disseminated on a limited basis, it was never utilized broadly within these organizations. One of the executives remarked: "It doesn't do me or the company any good for me to be the only advocate and teacher of this new approach." Analysis of these cases indicated that insufficient attention was given early in the change process to locating or developing other champions who could then act as agents of implementation.

In this respect, it is important to note that these champions need not be senior executives. In fact, Allen (1971) has shown that respected people at lower levels often turn out to be influential advocates, not because they act from a position of authority but rather because they possess the authority of knowledge. This point was grasped by Motorola executives in their quality improvement endeavors when they saw learning leap forward after they created a cadre of quality advocates spread throughout the company. In subsequent change efforts as many as 300 advocates were identified and enlisted to help develop and use a new approach prior to attempting large-scale implementation. These individuals were gathered in groups to build a supportive coalition and to become empowered to act.

Involved Leadership

Strong leadership is often a key factor in driving knowledge acquisition; from any level of the organization it sends a clear message about what is important to learn. Good leaders grasp this intuitively and frequently know how to get people to attend to an issue. However, leaders often fail to understand how important it is for them to be involved in knowledge dissemination and utilization. They then find that knowledge developed or created at great expense is not broadly used nor does it serve as a springboard for application in new settings. For example, almost every organization that has embarked on broad educational endeavors reports relatively poor use of what people presumably learned. We are told over and over that knowledge dissemination and knowledge utilization are more problematic than knowledge acquisition. Often the problem is that leaders are less involved at those later stages.

Much has been said about the importance of leadership in setting a vision that mobilizes enhanced performance. Our findings indicate that merely creating vision is not enough. For truly assimilated, actionable learning to occur, leaders need to be early developers and students of the knowledge. They must engage in hands-on implementation of the vision, including being visible in the bowels of the organization as a model for the learning effort. In short, at any level of an organization it makes a huge difference if those in leadership positions can demonstrate that they have learned what they want others to learn.

At Motorola, CEO Bob Galvin not only drove the quality vision but was a student in the first seminars designed to learn about it and made it the first item to be reported to him by his division executives in their monthly meetings. Much-admired WalMart CEO David Glass, believing that little constructive work is accomplished at company headquarters, spends two or three days each week at stores and warehouses. Employees are able to call him at home and are often passed on to his hotel room when he is in the field. Mike Walsh of Tenneco (formerly of Union Pacific Railroad) customarily met with groups of people at all levels of the firm in what Peters (1992) calls "conversation." This kind of involvement need not be restricted to senior executives; it can also be found at lower levels of organizations. Japanese managers at all levels are known for their hands-on involvement.

Many leaders, particularly senior management, may have some difficulty adopting this style, for it goes against the more detached manner that has been preached and taught to them for some decades. With the advent of scientific management it became fashionable to exhort managers to direct most of their effort to planning and analysis and to stay hands-off at the operational level. We now know that this aloofness prevents gathering the information they need so that it instead must filter up to them. Thus, Involved Leadership means learning for the leader as well as providing a stimulus for others to learn. One result is that leadership is no longer vested in a single individual or executive position. Rather, it is a trait exhibited both vertically and horizontally throughout any organization.

Systems Perspective

This factor has to do with the ability to think in terms of whole systems and the interdependence of parts. When managers lack a Systems Perspective their actions often lead to unanticipated consequences. Time lags and delays between the parts of a system mean that long-term results usually differ from short-term ones. Managers cannot learn when they focus on short-term results and ignore the long-term consequences of their actions. Peter Senge considers the "discipline" of Systems Perspective to be the one that integrates all the others in his five-factor model of the learning organization.

As with Involved Leadership, lack of a strong Systems Perspective is a barrier to successful dissemination and utilization of knowledge.

Even if good leadership helps to produce knowledge acquisition in particular areas, robust learning will not occur without this perspective. Organizational learning is limited when staff cannot recognize the relationships among processes, structures, and dispersed actions.

Despite its importance, Systems Perspective is relatively lacking in most organizations. MIC and Motorola are structured so that boundaries between groups and functions tend to be very rigid. In recent years both have tried to develop a Systems Perspective, MIC as a response to unexpected problems related to the October 1987 drop in the stock market and Motorola due to difficulties in selling large-scale systems (as opposed to discrete products). At Fiat Auto and Ford Motor Company, the lack of systems integration in new product development led to uncompetitive cycle time in bringing new cars to market. Both took a systems approach to understand the consequences of their structure and internal processes in causing this delay. As a result, they changed their design processes to simultaneous or concurrent engineering. To reduce the time to market of new products, functions now work in parallel rather than sequentially.

Many organizations have developed large-scale educational programs to address their lack of Systems Perspective. Some of these are designed to teach the principles of system dynamics of the kind pioneered by Jay Forrester at MIT's Sloan School of Management. The well-known "beer game" developed by John Sterman at MIT is a valuable teaching device to show how lack of Systems Perspective can get an organization into trouble. Other interventions are designed to get people from relevant parts of the organization to work on actual problems requiring a systemwide solution. Unilever, Motorola, and Grace Cocoa are among organizations that make use of this approach.

The Role of Facilitating Factors

As normative elements, the ten Facilitating Factors represent the conditions or practices that make organizations learn. In effect, they provide the reasons or incentives for organizational learning. Exactly what gets learned and how much depends on how the presence of Facilitating Factors in an organization combines with its Learning Orientations. Both sets of elements are needed to understand any organization's learning capability. In the next several chapters we explore how to use this framework to build learning capability.

We conclude this chapter with a description of the Facilitating Factors at work in one corporation.

Case Study:
Organizational Learning at Investment Funds Group

Investment Funds Group (IFG) is a division of Mutual Investment Corporation (MIC), the pseudonym of a large American financial services company that manages more than $40 billion worth of various securities. IFG staff manage over $9 billion in fourteen different mutual funds by investing in fixed-income securities. At MIC there is a shared belief that understanding investment markets requires constant vigilance and that being a good analyst or portfolio manager involves both art (intuition) and science (analysis). An underlying assumption is that there is no one correct way to manage funds, that despite good research and investment skills some uncertainty exists about investment markets. Consistent with this assumption, high value is placed on the acceptance of diverse opinions so that MIC does not simply "follow the herd."

Why Organizational Learning Occurs

There are several dominant reasons why organizational learning occurs at IFG. The first is generic to the industry of which IFG is a part; the others derive from MIC's organizational culture.

Presence of clear performance measures. IFG operates in an industry where performance is a public fact. The nature of the investment business readily lends itself to measurement, so the performance of IFG mutual funds is tracked on both a daily and a longitudinal basis. Knowledge about performance is analyzed not only internally by MIC but externally by service companies that sell such information to investors. This monitoring of performance provides ongoing feedback on IFG performance relative to that of the competition.

Performance implications, performance significance. The invest-ment industry is not the only one that has clear measures of perfor-mance. What makes such measures important at IFG is that there are specific implications of performance for staff compensation and the market appeal of MIC's products. IFG staff frequently refer to MIC as being performance-driven, because performance provides a clear rationale for investment and personnel decisions, the size of client accounts, and staff compensation.

Special effort to improve performance. IFG's inability several years ago to perform as well as other MIC divisions led MIC management to take several initiatives. First, in pointing out the relatively poor per-formance of IFG, MIC leadership called upon senior IFG staff to seek ways to reduce the gap. This mandate legitimized the need for orga-nizational change and to incorporate learning (that is, utilize knowl-edge from experience) into operations. Second, IFG was provided access to internal resources that had proven valuable in achieving high levels of performance in other parts of MIC. Subsequently, new staff brought into IFG became a resource for knowledge acquisition.

This case suggests that learning occurs at IFG because it is rel-atively high in several Facilitating Factors. First, there is high regard for measurement (Concern for Measurement); fund performance is tracked every day and short- and long-term results are monitored. The high expectations of MIC corporate staff ensure the steady pres-ence of a Performance Gap; as performance improves and reduces the gap, goals or expectations are raised to expand it again. Lead-ership at multiple organizational levels is involved in promoting learn-ing. MIC's CEO is an advocate of *kaizen* (Japanese for "continuous improvement") management practices; IFG's chief executive and fund managers all promote learning in their own groups. By drawing upon resources from other parts of MIC, IFG demonstrated a high empha-sis on Scanning Imperative and Operational Variety.

Part II

Helping Organizations Learn

5

Recognizing Your Organization's Learning Portfolio

In the previous three chapters we presented our two-part framework of organizational learning capability. This framework combines both the descriptive (Learning Orientations) and prescriptive (Facilitating Factors) elements that together represent learning capability in organizations. Before discussing how this framework can guide the building of such capability, we need to add one more integrating piece that comes from the *developmental perspective* of organizational learning.

Developmental Perspective: Learning Styles

The developmental perspective contributes the notion that organizations have different learning styles that vary over time. Organizations build learning capability when they get better at working their style or change it so their style matches the demands of their business. This chapter describes what a learning style is, shows the characteristics of eight different styles, and explains how learning styles constitute a firm's learning portfolio (DiBella, Nevis, and Gould, 1996). The case at the end of the chapter describes Fiat Auto's efforts to alter its learning styles.

Organizational learning style is a function of how organizations learn. In our integrated framework, how they learn is represented by the seven Learning Orientations (or fourteen approaches to learning). By combining the LOrs in pairs, it is possible to identify distinctive styles of learning. Such styles do not indicate how well an organization is learning nor do they judge the value of what is learned, but they do indicate a great deal about what is learned and how. In effect, an organization's pattern of learning orientations reflects its learning style (Srivastva, 1983). Orientations can be used to generate a composite picture of an organization's learning style and to suggest directions to build on or change that style.

Learning style represents an organization's acquired capability. To use that capability for competitive advantage, organizations must first be able to recognize what it consists of; that is the starting point for deciding on strategic action to change, augment, or enhance the style. Rather than presuming no existing competence and the need to build it from the bottom up, managers should work with and from what already exists.

In recent years, the work of Howard Gardner (1993) and Daniel Goleman (1995) has shown that understanding the learning capability of individuals requires more than just testing their intelligence quotients. Learning and intelligence are multidimensional concepts that cannot be tested with a single measure. Reliance on single measures simplifies reality but, more critically, devalues ways of learning and forms of intelligence that deviate from social norms. A consequence is conformity, which may make it easier to control children in a classroom but does harm to those whose ways of being, thinking, and learning happens to be different. And different ways of thinking produce innovation and the "out-of-the-box" thinking needed to see possibilities where others see only constraints and opportunities where others see only crises.

Much as individuals learn in different ways (Kolb, 1979), so do organizations. To some extent these differences are a function of the diverse environments in which organizations must operate. For example, in stable environments with established products like ketchup or ice cubes, what and how organizations learn will be very different from what occurs in industries that are volatile and involve new products or evolving technologies, such as computer hardware and software. Learning differences between organizations also occur as a result of differences in history, culture, size, and age. New entrepreneurial firms are apt to learn differently from larger established firms. This creates opportunities, as for Apple in the 1960s and 1970s to take market share away from IBM.

The figures in this chapter are examples of how our seven LOrs can be combined to identify learning styles. Each LOr represents a continuum of two contrasting approaches. When two LOrs are juxtaposed against one another, the result is a two-by-two matrix. Each of the four boxes in a matrix represents a learning style. Most organizations have one dominant learning style but may also employ other styles from time to time. Figure 5.1 shows four learning styles as determined by Knowledge Source and Learning Scope. Following is a description of each of the four.

1. Correction: Internal Knowledge Source and Incremental Learning Scope

When organizations learn from their own operations and use that knowledge incrementally, they make corrections to existing products or systems. This style of learning is probably the most used, if not the most talked about. When organizations implement their strategies or run their assembly lines, they may discover that their actions only partially achieve their goals or result in negative consequences, as when a train derails or automobiles are assembled improperly. In such cases, they adjust what they do to avoid re-experiencing the negative outcome. The thesaurus contains many words for an act or event that can lead to corrective learning: failure, error, mistake, miscalculation, defect, flaw, imperfection, and blemish. Through our own experience, we recognize a need to make adjustments or recalculations in what we are doing. We learn because in some way our experience does not match our desire, so we adjust or correct what we are already doing. Total quality management (TQM), with its emphasis on continuous improvement, is a well-known method used for this learning style.

Figure 5.1.   Learning Style Matrix No. 1

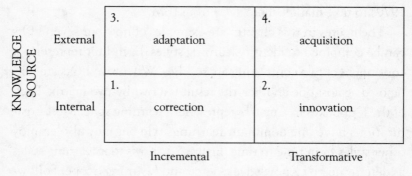

Learning Style as Determined by:

KNOWLEDGE SOURCE AND LEARNING SCOPE

2. Innovation: Internal Knowledge Source and Transformative Learning Scope

When organizations learn from their own operations and use that knowledge transformatively, they create product or process innovations. For years large American firms, such as 3M, Xerox, and Motorola, as well as many entrepreneurial start-up firms have made their fortunes by developing new technologies or product ideas. For example, many household and business office items that we now take for granted were major innovations when they were introduced: fax machines, compact disc players, microwave ovens, Velcro. Firms learn by using their own competence and capabilities to generate products that transform the market.

3. Adaptation: External Knowledge Source and Incremental Learning Scope

Adaptation occurs when organizations make incremental changes or improvements to knowledge acquired externally. Japanese firms are noted for this ability to take basic ideas developed elsewhere and use them to improve existing products or to develop related products. In the United States there is a cultural bias against adaptation; innovation is regarded as a more prestigious and glamorous way to grab market share. However, the experience not only of many Japanese companies but American companies as well (for example, IBM's adaptation of Univac's computer ideas) indicates that companies can be very profitable if they employ this learning style as a key strategy.

4. Acquisition: External Knowledge Source and Transformative Learning Scope

Investing in learning activities, such as the research and development needed to create innovation, takes commitment and persistence. Some firms are better at focusing on what they already do than at focusing on learning, for learning is its own form of work. However, some firms have resources that allow them to acquire what has been learned by others and then incorporate that learning into their own operations. To utilize external knowledge that is transformative involves some amount of acquisition. Corporate buyouts, mergers, and acquisitions are corporate-level strategies that, in effect, allow firms to purchase the capabilities developed by others.

In our research, we found organizations that are successful in using these different learning styles. IFG, which is very internal with regard to Knowledge Source and mainly incremental with regard to Learning Scope, has a predominant style of learning that stresses corrective action. As fund managers learn about the results of their investment decisions, they correct their choices to maximize their financial returns.

Correction is IFG's dominant learning style, but it also engages in others from time to time. For example, portfolio management is a well-established business practice at which IFG has been very successful. Fund managers have little time or interest in transformative learning when they are managing millions and in some cases billions of investment dollars daily. Sometimes IFG competitors exhibit new ways of making investment decisions; perhaps one of their analysts develops a new econometric model with accompanying software that better predicts market behavior. IFG's parent firm, MIC, has large financial resources of its own, so its usual response is to purchase the new software or simply hire its designer. In effect, IFG uses acquisition as a learning style to gain new knowledge and competence.

Fiat Auto's Direzione Technica is evenly balanced in its approaches to Knowledge Source and Learning Scope. The result is a set of styles. Fiat Auto's acquisitions of Lancia and Alfa Romeo have been its principal source of innovation. Through customer feedback, Fiat Auto learns what car components need correcting. A management initiative to benchmark Fiat Auto against other world-class auto producers was a way to generate knowledge externally. It exhibited its skill at adaptation by subsequently integrating these "best practices" developed elsewhere into its own operations.

Firms may employ different learning styles at different historical points. When EDF began to build its infrastructure of nuclear power plants in the 1970s, it used a standard design developed in the United States by Westinghouse. This learning strategy combined the learning styles of adaptation and acquisition. EDF then focused on making incremental changes to the design of its plants based on its own operating experience, reflecting a learning style that emphasized correction. Now, in the 1990s, EDF is building an innovative, entirely new series of plants based on its own knowledge.

Motorola is evolving toward a balanced set of styles. It appears able to use both internal and external sources of knowledge and to be both innovative and adaptive. Perhaps this is why it is perceived to be an excellent example of a learning organization ("Companies That Train Best," 1993; "Motorola: Training for the Millenium," 1994).

The companies we studied demonstrate that business success is not dependent on a particular learning style. Organizations can be successful using one style or a set of styles. This statement seems obvious enough. However, in their rush to implement some formula for success some managers will forget it and try to emulate whatever is in vogue. For example, in American business culture an innovative learning style is more glamorous and more valued than a corrective one. Yet in some situations a corrective style is clearly to be preferred. At a nuclear power plant, for example, control room staff should not be in an innovative mode when the reactor is fully operational. No one would accept the consequences of innovative learning that led to an unknown or cataclysmic outcome. Also, entire industries could not have been built and stabilized had not learning transitioned from a phase of innovative to corrective learning. For example, innovative learning was needed to develop jet aircraft, but it took and still takes corrective learning to achieve acceptable safety standards. Thus there is no universally right or wrong learning style. A learning style represents organizational learning capability of some sort; whether it is the right style for a particular firm or situation depends on overall corporate strategy, market conditions, and performance demands.

Figure 5.2 shows four more learning styles, as determined by Knowledge Reserve and Dissemination Mode.

1. Role Modeling: Informal Dissemination Mode and Personal Knowledge Reserve

When knowledge is seen in personal terms but disseminated in an informal manner, learning occurs through role modeling or social emulation. Many firms rely on specialized knowledge or skills that are intuitive or cannot be made explicit. Sometimes that knowledge is retained by individuals and can only be disseminated directly from one person to another. Through mentoring relationships or observation, individuals learn from one another. The learning is not imposed but acquired or shared through informal, often subconscious means. By doing as others do, we learn from them in discrete ways.

Figure 5.2.   Learning Style Matrix No. 2

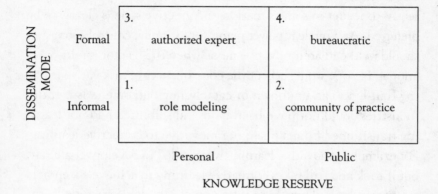

Learning Style as Determined by:

DISSEMINATION MODE AND KNOWLEDGE RESERVE

		Personal	Public
DISSEMINATION MODE	Formal	3. authorized expert	4. bureaucratic
	Informal	1. role modeling	2. community of practice

KNOWLEDGE RESERVE

2. Communities of Practice:
Informal Dissemination Mode and Public Knowledge Reserve

"Communities of practice" is a learning style that involves public or collective learning in an informal manner and that is consistent with a broader learning theory (Lave and Wenger, 1991). Based on research with Xerox machine repair technicians, John Seeley Brown (Brown and Duguid, 1991) likewise came to the conclusion that all learning is, in essence, social. We learn with, through, and from others. When people swap stories about their experience they share what they have each learned, but in the process they can also create new learning by collectively generating insights that they could not have produced alone. Communities of practice provide social contexts for the informal dissemination of knowledge that can lead to new, collaborative learning (Wenger, 1996).

3. Authorized Expert: Formal Dissemination Mode and Personal Knowledge Reserve

When knowledge is seen in personal terms and disseminated in a formal manner, organizations rely on authorized experts to accumulate learning. When staff want to learn how to do something, they do not go to a procedures manual but to the resident company expert who has a reputation for knowing the subject. Often such experts are placed in positions where part of their job is to share their expertise with others; in this way, the staff member is formally acknowledged to be the expert. When solicited, the expert's advice is followed prescriptively.

4. Bureaucratic: Formal Dissemination Mode and Public Knowledge Reserve

A bureaucratic style of learning reflects a formal method of disseminating knowledge that applies to all, often in the form of written procedures. The technology in some industries is well known and well specified, perhaps because it developed over time through the precise work of many. How-tos are carefully documented to avoid mistakes or to pass on to others simple instructions on how to perform tasks. Such instructions are universally available so anyone can benefit from the learning of others. For example, procedures for maintaining aircraft engines are highly specific to ensure safe airline operation and to conform to industry and FAA safety standards. Such procedures are modified over time as experience is gained in how maintenance affects engine performance.

In the sites we studied we saw evidence of all these learning styles. We also saw that some organizations had a dominant style and others practiced a set of styles. At IFG, to formally embed lessons learned about investing and specify them in a procedure manual would be anathema to the company's entrepreneurial and individualistic culture. Instead learning takes place through role modeling and, increasingly, by having fund managers participate in communal meetings to share information. In contrast, when EDF generates knowledge through the analysis of a critical incident, the result is often a change in procedures. This form of bureaucratic learning ensures that everyone has access to the proper way to perform so that incidents do not recur. At Fiat Auto, Direzione Technica is attempting to change its learning styles from those based on formal mechanisms for disseminating knowledge to informal ones. For example, by working in collocation engineers increase their chance of learning collaboratively as a community of practice.

Developing Your Company's Learning Portfolio

Our research revealed that some organizations have a dominant learning style. Many more use a variety of styles, each providing some learning capability. Also, we found different organizational learning styles in different parts of the same company. Perhaps this is not surprising; after all, we might expect that a group of engineers would learn differently together than would a group, team, or department of accountants or marketing experts. Yet the power of the normative perspective—that learning should occur in a particular prescriptive way—often crowds out this recognition.

One way to accept the diversity of learning styles involves thinking of a company as having a portfolio of styles. Companies with a large portfolio of styles are apt to have multiple competences and a greater capacity to adapt to change than companies that rely on a single learning style. By focusing on a company's learning portfolio in its entirety we reorient ourselves from wondering whether the company has the right learning style to considering the complementarity of its styles. Instead of evaluating the style of a particular part of a company, we take a systems view to consider the synergistic possibilities. Recognizing the presence of multiple styles within a company can also explain intergroup conflicts and barriers to learning. If different parts of a company learn in different ways, it is highly unlikely that knowledge will be transferred across functional or project boundaries (Schein, 1996). Once we recognize such differences, we can manage them as a potential source of competitive advantage.

The learning styles identified in this chapter can be used to understand the scope of an organization's learning portfolio. Often there is an overemphasis or specialization in one style of learning, as reflected in the Learning Orientations, whereas the most advantageous position for a company may be to have access to multiple learning styles to take advantage of different market circumstances or competences. Managers need to understand the fit between an organization's learning style, its product or service, and its industrial environment.

By identifying existing learning capabilities it is possible to establish a starting point for organization development interventions. For example, organizations may choose to change their Learning Orientations (and hence their culture). Ulrich, Jick, and Von Gunow (1993) argue that to enhance learning requires a fundamental change in culture, but our research indicates that is not necessarily the case. The effort at Fiat Auto's Direzione Technica does involve an effort to change corporate culture. Yet organizations may enhance their learning by improving what they already do well, an approach taken by IFG and EDF. Improving what one already does is a less threatening way of developing learning capability and, in the case of nuclear power, a less dangerous way.

One possible reason why managers often ignore existing capabilities is their attention to the plea that organizations must first unlearn before they can learn (Hedberg, 1981; McGill and Slocum, 1993). However, to develop learning capability organizations must distinguish unlearning *what* they know and do from *how* they learn as represented by their learning portfolio. Managers can then make more informed assessments about how present capabilities realize or inhibit learning and whether barriers to improved performance exist because of what is being learned or because of how learning takes place.

If one accepts the potential of the two-part model of normative (Facilitating Factors) and descriptive (Learning Orientations) elements, it follows that two general directions are indicated for building organizational learning. One direction is to embrace the existing style and try to improve its effectiveness. This is the strategy of actualizing a fundamental part of the culture to the fullest extent possible. For example, a firm that emphasizes adaptation rather than innovation could accept this with heightened awareness of its value. One that has benefited from heavy learning investments in the "make" side of the value chain would see the value of this and decide to build further on it. The work would then be to look at the Facilitating Factors and select two or three to improve upon.

The second option is to change the learning style or enlarge the organization's portfolio of styles. In this option, an organization would look at its pattern of LOrs and attempt to move to some other point along the continuum of one or several of them. For example, the organization could make more learning investments at a different part of the value chain or try to be more of an innovator if it is now more of an adapter. These are different changes than those involved in enhancing the Facilitating Factors, so the change tactics will be different; some will be seen as an attack upon the organization's basic values. It may be possible to get around this by advocating a move toward more balance between the two poles of an LOr; the existing style would be supported and the "new look" would be advocated as a supplementary measure. Chapters Six, Seven, and Eight go into more detail on how to focus on Learning Orientations and Facilitating Factors to build learning capability.

Case Study: Fiat Auto's Learning Portfolio

Fiat Auto currently designs, manufactures, and markets automobiles worldwide under a variety of trademarks including Fiat, Lancia, and Alfa Romeo. Staffed by approximately 3,000 managers and professionals, Direzione Technica (DT) is Fiat Auto's engineering division responsible for the design of new automobiles. DT is organized into functional departments that specialize in particular aspects of car design, such as body style or engines.

Fiat once produced vehicles under the Fiat trademark only. Subsequently it acquired Lancia and then Alfa Romeo. Each trademark was produced in separate companies, which gave Fiat Auto a product-focused organization structure. In 1991 the three car companies were reorganized as Fiat Auto into a functionally based structure with a heavy emphasis on project management. Trademark models are designed by new-product development teams that reside in staff groups *(piattaformas)* responsible for the new models of a certain size or cost, such as subcompact or luxury. Staff from functional units are assigned to the *piattaformas* on a full-time basis to develop new models.

In 1989 Fiat Auto had one of its most successful years ever. In the same year its CEO authorized benchmarking studies to compare its performance to that of other world automobile manufacturers and a few consumer durable goods companies. Approximately fifty of Fiat's top managers participated in this study by visiting other firms and their plants worldwide. The study group discovered that not only was the marketplace changing due to different consumer tastes and expectations but the processes whereby firms design and manufacture products were also rapidly changing. The group became convinced that although Fiat Auto was having a successful year, unless it changed how it worked and how it learned it would lose its ability to compete with global companies.

One of the process changes DT made was to simultaneous engineering. New-product development teams now work together in common, open areas to facilitate communication and coordination. Staff from the Direzione Technica and from other Fiat Auto divisions also assigned to the *piattaformas,* such as manufacturing and marketing, also work in collocation. Where engineers and other functional staff once worked sequentially on related tasks, now they work concurrently—in parallel rather than in series. With this form of "simultaneous engineering," new models are completed without the time delays that occurred when components were designed sequentially or when newly designed components had to pass from function to function.

In describing the roots of Fiat's organizational culture, staff often refer to Italy's tradition of paternalistic, religious, and militaristic organization forms. Particular reference is made to the heavy reliance on authority that stems from rigid, hierarchical structures and the acceptance of formal authority. There is significant concern at DT that Fiat's traditional culture generated too much of a Taylorian division between those staff who did the thinking and those who acted. During the last two years DT has learned about making the transition to a more open and flexible organization. This transition is reflected in the desire to shift the style of management from "*capo*" (head, commander) to "leader." In the former, the framework is to command and obey; in the new framework of management the focus is on cooperation and integration.

Discrete projects aimed at improvement and learning have been completed or are still under way. Management's aim is to spawn institutionalized processes that facilitate continuous improvement. It is expected that changing the culture, structure, and management style at DT will accomplish this. Among the formal mechanisms to spawn learning is the use of Total Quality Planning (TQP) to identify areas needing improvement. TQP is required of all organizational units to identify both product and process issues that can be improved upon.

Staff also expect learning to occur through the very mechanisms whereby work is accomplished. DT's functional departments learn through the acquisition of "know-how engineering" and the establishment and improvement of "shelf engineering." Each functional unit is also expected to build a *memoria technica,* a database containing knowledge about components and processes. Learning also occurs in the *piattaformas* through the application and utilization of know-how engineering in car design. In solving design problems for specific models, functional staff may generate solutions that, once communicated back to the function, may subsequently be applied in the design of other models.

The experiences at Fiat Auto indicate a concerted effort to build learning capability by enhancing and extending DT's learning portfolio. Fiat has learned through acquisition (of Lancia and Alfa Romeo), through adaptation (of best practices obtained through its benchmarking studies), and through correction via its TQP process. Now shifts in work process will create new learning capabilities. For example, the *memoria technica* represents a bureaucratic learning style. The shift to concurrent engineering will create communities of practice, and the change in leadership style represents a shift from a learning style of authorized expert to role modeling.

6

Developing a Learning Strategy

In Chapters Three, Four, and Five, we discussed the Learning Orientations (LOrs), Facilitating Factors (FFs), and learning styles that represent an organization's learning capability. The seventeen FF and LOr elements identify important structures, processes, and characteristics that influence the nature of what is learned and how it is learned. They form the building blocks or pattern of elements that begin to describe what we call a learning system and its unique profile of strengths and value preferences that define organizational learning. (A learning profile is not the same as learning styles or the learning portfolio we described in the last chapter. Rather, it represents an organization in terms of both FFs and LOrs, whereas learning styles are determined solely by LOrs.) Presumably, if an organization possesses awareness of its profile and its impact on performance effectiveness, it can make some decisions about how to improve its learning capability. This chapter and the one following are designed to help in the enhancement of this awareness and to suggest actions for improvement.

The Organizational Learning Profile

On the basis of our research and experience at building organizational learning capability, we created the Organizational Learning Profile, a tool that provides a picture of an organization's unique

Figure 6.1.   Organizational Learning Profile

LEARNING
ORIENTATIONS

	MOSTLY	MORE	EVEN	MORE	MOSTLY	
1. Knowledge Source	INTERNAL					EXTERNAL
2. Content-Process Focus	CONTENT					PROCESS
3. Knowledge Reserve	PERSONAL					PUBLIC
4. Dissemination Mode	FORMAL					INFORMAL
5. Learning Scope	INCREMENTAL					TRANSFORMATIVE
6. Value-Chain Focus	DESIGN-MAKE					MARKET-DELIVER
7. Learning Focus	INDIVIDUAL					GROUP

FACILITATING FACTORS

	Little evidence to support this factor		Some evidence to support this factor			Extensive evidence to support this factor	
	1	2	3	4	5	6	7
1. Scanning Imperative							
2. Performance Gap							
3. Concern for Measurement							
4. Organizational Curiosity							
5. Climate of Openness							
6. Continuous Education							
7. Operational Variety							
8. Multiple Advocates							
9. Involved Leadership							
10. Systems Perspective							

Unit Being Profiled _____

Names of Participants _____

Company and Phone Number _____

Date of Profile _____

learning system. This snapshot of the current situation can be used to develop a projection of where the unit would like to move in the future. Figure 6.1 shows the profile and how it organizes the seventeen elements into the categories of Learning Orientations and Facilitating Factors. Note that the former are measured in terms of polar categories that are the ends of a continuum. This reflects the descriptive nature of these dimensions and the goal of looking at each end or approach as desirable. The FFs are measured in terms of how much of the element is present, in keeping with their normative nature.

Once a profile of current learning capability is obtained, an obvious next step is to determine what might be a more desirable pattern of capabilities, given the needs of the organization or firm and its particular strategic thrust. Strategy and learning are thus brought into alignment. Darling and Hennessy (1995) refer to this as "charting a corporate learning strategy." This involves selection of several variables to address in efforts to improve organizational effectiveness.

Assessing Organizational Learning Capability

Implications can be drawn from an organization's position on each of the seventeen elements. The organization may wish to examine the factors that support or determine each position and analyze how it got to this state. It then may decide that a current position is the most appropriate place to be, or that it is not appropriate or desirable and some change should be made.

As a way of learning to assess a profile and use it to develop a learning strategy, it will be useful to look briefly at some comparative data to see the way unique patterns develop. These data were obtained through intensive group analyses conducted by us with members of organizational units through use of the Organizational Learning Inventory, an assessment device we developed for this purpose.

Figure 6.2 presents profiles of two manufacturing organizations. "A" is a well-known, highly successful pharmaceutical firm considered by many to be one of the best in its field. "B" is a well-known and highly successful company in the electronics business. Each is but one of many manufacturing units in its firm. There are similarities in the two profiles but also significant differences. With regard to Learning Orientations, both emphasize an incremental Learning Scope and a formal Dissemination Mode. However, "A" is more focused on external Knowledge Source, public Knowledge Reserve, market-deliver Value-Chain Focus, and group Learning Focus. With regard to Facilitating Factors, "A" has greater Organizational Curiosity, Climate of Openness, and Multiple Advocates. It ranks lower than "B," however, on Involved Leadership and Concern for Measurement. Both are relatively low in Operational Variety and Systems Perspective.

Analysis of the two profiles suggests that the dominant learning styles of "A" are adaptation and bureaucratic, whereas "B" uses correction and authorized experts. The learning strengths of "A" are built on an outward orientation and a reasonably strong customer focus. "A" is also more open and informal inside the firm, with leadership only moderately involved in implementation of learning initiatives. "B" apparently makes greater learning investments in internal knowledge production than does "A." It has a relatively high Scanning Imperative, awareness of Performance Gaps, and high Concern for Measurement, all of which indicate study of the outside world in a measured way. "B," however, exhibits low Organizational Curiosity, low Climate of Openness, and relatively low use of Multiple Advocates, suggesting that a great deal of information comes into the unit but does not necessarily lead to experimentation and frame-breaking thinking. The strong evidence for Involved Leadership at "B" together with relatively low presence of Multiple Advocates suggests more of a "top-down" approach than at "A," which shows an opposite pattern on these two Facilitating Factors. Finally, both "A" and "B" are quite low on Systems Perspective, raising a question as to how well learning is directed to issues of integration and interdependence. Members of both these units

Figure 6.2. Organizational Learning Profiles of Units in Two Different Firms

LEARNING
ORIENTATIONS

		MOSTLY	MORE	EVEN	MORE	MOSTLY	
1. Knowledge Source	INTERNAL		B		A		EXTERNAL
2. Content-Process Focus	CONTENT		B	A			PROCESS
3. Knowledge Reserve	PERSONAL		B		A		PUBLIC
4. Dissemination Mode	FORMAL		AB				INFORMAL
5. Learning Scope	INCREMENTAL	AB					TRANSFORMATIVE
6. Value-Chain Focus	DESIGN-MAKE			B	A		MARKET-DELIVER
7. Learning Focus	INDIVIDUAL		B	A			GROUP

FACILITATING FACTORS

	Little evidence to support this factor		Some evidence to support this factor			Extensive evidence to support this factor	
	1	2	3	4	5	6	7
1. Scanning Imperative				A	B		
2. Performance Gap		A		B			
3. Concern for Measurement			A		B		
4. Organizational Curiosity		B		A			
5. Climate of Openness		B		A			
6. Continuous Education			B	A			
7. Operational Variety		BA					
8. Multiple Advocates			B			A	
9. Involved Leadership			A		B		
10. Systems Perspective		BA					

A = Manufacturing Division, Pharmaceutical
B = Manufacturing Unit, High-Tech Firm

Unit Being Profiled _____

Names of Participants _____
Company and Phone Number _____
Date of Profile _____

report that many decisions are made in their firm that do not consider the impact on manufacturing. They see R&D and marketing as being more highly valued than manufacturing.

From a strategic point of view, one of the first questions to address is whether each of these units should build on its strengths and enhance an already noteworthy competence or whether they might benefit more by moving in a different direction on the Learning Orientations, enhancing select Facilitating Factors, or both. We will deal with such questions in later sections of the book.

Figure 6.3 presents profiles for three units in one company. Analysis of the profiles shows that all three are oriented to looking internally for knowledge development and that they prefer to invest in proprietary R&D as opposed to adapting the knowledge of others. Surprisingly, considering that this manufacturing company is built around process technology, the managers in all units agreed that they were heavily focused on the end product and gave only minimal attention to building process technology into a core competence. Clearly, improving the design and development of the product is more valued than producing and marketing it. Unit C is interesting in that it sees itself as more advanced in Scanning Imperative and transformational Learning Scope. This unit, which specializes in R&D, is considered a maverick by its division. Taken with the personal Knowledge Reserve, relatively low Systems Perspective, and low interest in using measurement for learning (Concern for Measurement), we see the rudiments of a loose and lively approach to learning based on an assumption that it will somehow emerge. The learning portfolio of all three units is fairly narrow, with major emphasis placed on correction and authorized experts.

Unit A has the greatest Involved Leadership of the three but very low presence of Multiple Advocates. This suggests a current learning strategy where learning initiatives are centered in a small number of leaders who may expect knowledge to be transmitted broadly by organized education and dissemination vehicles. With a balance between design-make and market-deliver in Value-Chain

Focus, high Concern for Measurement, and a high level of Continuous Education, Unit A appears to be a more conservative group with a moderate Systems Perspective. The overall pattern is quite different from that of Unit C.

Unit B, although similar to Units A and C in numerous ways, is noteworthy for having low Involved Leadership but heavy use of Multiple Advocates. This group is also the most oriented to group or team learning and to incremental learning. It does not have a wide lens in scanning or well-developed Organizational Curiosity. We can only assume that the unit, which has manufacturing responsibilities, has learned to operate and learn in a relatively organized way, with few surprises or deviations in its output. This style appears well-suited for a line operation with clear production quotas. The learning profile allows room for people to initiate and champion new ideas, but at a relatively mundane level. Hardly an imaginative or risk-taking group, it nonetheless creates and disseminates knowledge within the limits it has set for itself. From other sources, we learn that the senior leader of the group is absent much of the time due to special assignments elsewhere.

At this point, we have a picture of the current situation in the units depicted in Figures 6.2 and 6.3. The next task in developing a learning strategy is to have these units create a profile of desired capabilities. While a unit may decide to remain as is, we have never seen a group that did not want to change in some way in order to improve its learning. If we look at the profiles of the three units just described, we can see how they might want to change. For example, Unit A can ask itself how it can leverage its stability into a higher level of performance. It can look at its strategic thrust to see if its essential conservatism will hamper initiatives that involve working from a new paradigm, such as turning its production system "upside down" in an attempt to respond to competitive pressures to lower costs and improve delivery times. More specifically, it can look simultaneously at its relatively low Organizational Curiosity, Climate of Openness, and Multiple Advocates, as well as

Figure 6.3. Organizational Learning Profiles of Three Units in the Same Firm

LEARNING
ORIENTATIONS

		MOSTLY	MORE	EVEN	MORE	MOSTLY	
1. Knowledge Source	INTERNAL		ABC				EXTERNAL
2. Content-Process Focus	CONTENT	BC		A			PROCESS
3. Knowledge Reserve	PERSONAL		ABC				PUBLIC
4. Dissemination Mode	FORMAL		AB	C			INFORMAL
5. Learning Scope	INCREMENTAL	B	A	C			TRANSFORMATIVE
6. Value-Chain Focus	DESIGN-MAKE	C	B	A			MARKET-DELIVER
7. Learning Focus	INDIVIDUAL		C	A	B		GROUP

FACILITATING FACTORS	Little evidence to support this factor			Some evidence to support this factor		Extensive evidence to support this factor	
	1	2	3	4	5	6	7
1. Scanning Imperative		B	A		C		
2. Performance Gap				C	B	A	
3. Concern for Measurement			C	B			A
4. Organizational Curiosity		B	AC				
5. Climate of Openness			CAB				
6. Continuous Education					CB	A	
7. Operational Variety				BC	A		
8. Multiple Advocates		A				BC	
9. Involved Leadership	B			C		A	
10. Systems Perspective		BC		A			

A = TQM Administration and Planning
B = Manufacturing
C = Research and Development

Unit Being Profiled _____

Names of Participants _____
Company and Phone Number _____
Date of Profile _____

its Content Focus and internal orientation to Knowledge Source. It can raise a question as to whether the high degree of Involved Leadership unwittingly creates dependence among those lower in the organization. These are just some of the possible starting points.

By contrast, the strategy for Unit C might well entail a look at whether it has many initiatives under way (high Multiple Advocates) that are not integrated or leveraged due to a relatively low Systems Perspective.

Making Strategic Choices Using Profile Analysis

To show how actionable choices may follow from the analysis of a learning profile, we present two cases. The first case is a division of National Semiconductor Corporation. The second draws from a published case depicting use of our model at the Harvard University Law Library (Darling and Hennessy, 1995).

Case Study: National Semiconductor

One of the first organizations to make wide use of our model was National Semiconductor Corporation (NSC) at its facility in Maine. The initiative developed in 1993 out of a desire to quickly obtain a reliable picture of the organization's strengths and areas for improvement as NSC adapts to changes in its marketplace. It was part of a large-scale change effort supported by a new CEO who was hired to "turn the company around."

NSC has exceptional manufacturing ability, but leadership at the facility wanted to improve learning capability in shortening product development cycles and reducing development costs. Initially, learning profiles were developed for a baseline assessment of a group of forty engineers with diverse responsibilities and backgrounds. A second use was with a value delivery redesign team, which decided to focus on improvement in the Facilitating Factors. A third learning profile was developed with the director of a number of product lines and

40 of his approximately 160 staff members. The third use revealed interesting differences between the perceptions of senior management of the group and those of lower-level staff members. Figure 6.4 (pp. 112–113) presents these data. Note that the major differences are in Climate of Openness, Continuous Education, Multiple Advocates, and Systems Perspective. These results led the entire group to engage in an extensive analysis of underlying factors and corrective actions. Several action steps emerged and became part of NSC's overall change strategy.

Case Study: Harvard University Law Library

This application developed out of the desire of a law professor serving as head of the Harvard University Law Library to design a significant restructuring of the library, beginning in June 1995, as a means of learning how to provide service in "the new virtual marketplace of legal research." All ninety members of the library's staff were introduced to our model and five groups of about five people each completed an organizational learning profile of the library. The entire group then reviewed the data to make an assessment of where it would like to be on the seventeen elements to develop its learning capability and improve its effectiveness. Based on gaps between the present state and the desired state, the group selected four elements as critical for improving performance and an action plan for doing this. These were the elements seen as critical to success or showing readiness for change: Systems Perspective, Involved Leadership, group Learning Focus (that is, moving there from an individual Learning Focus), and formal dissemination (moving away from informal Dissemination Mode). In particular, it was felt that a certain looseness existed that inhibited a robust leverage of individual efforts. Thus, two Learning Orientations and two Facilitating Factors were chosen. Figure 6.5 (pp. 114–115) shows the learning profile developed by the entire group, and Figure 6.6 (p. 116) depicts the learning charter that emerged around the four elements and specific goals and behaviors to strengthen them.

Figure 6.4. Organizational Learning Profile of National Semiconductor Corporation

LEARNING
ORIENTATIONS

		MOSTLY	MORE	EVEN	MORE	MOSTLY	
1. Knowledge Source	INTERNAL		AC	B			EXTERNAL
2. Content-Process Focus	CONTENT	CA			B		PROCESS
3. Knowledge Reserve	PERSONAL	C	A	B			PUBLIC
4. Dissemination Mode	FORMAL		BA	C			INFORMAL
5. Learning Scope	INCREMENTAL		CA	B			TRANSFORMATIVE
6. Value-Chain Focus	DESIGN-MAKE	B		CA			MARKET-DELIVER
7. Learning Focus	INDIVIDUAL		CB	A			GROUP

FACILITATING FACTORS

	Little evidence to support this factor		Some evidence to support this factor			Extensive evidence to support this factor	
	1	2	3	4	5	6	7
1. Scanning Imperative		AB	C				
2. Performance Gap					BC	A	
3. Concern for Measurement				B		C	A
4. Organizational Curiosity					C	BA	
5. Climate of Openness		C		B		A	
6. Continuous Education		C		A		B	
7. Operational Variety		C		AB			
8. Multiple Advocates		C			A	B	
9. Involved Leadership				BA	C		
10. Systems Perspective			C	A			B

A = Management Team focusing on quality issues
B = Team of Redesign Engineers
C = Product Management Group

Unit Being Profiled _____

Names of Participants _____
Company and Phone Number _____
Date of Profile _____

Figure 6.5. Organizational Learning Profile of the Harvard University Law Library

LEARNING ORIENTATIONS

		MOSTLY	MORE	EVEN	MORE	MOSTLY	
1. Knowledge Source	INTERNAL		X				EXTERNAL
2. Content-Process Focus	CONTENT		X				PROCESS
3. Knowledge Reserve	PERSONAL	X					PUBLIC
4. Dissemination Mode	FORMAL				X		INFORMAL
5. Learning Scope	INCREMENTAL	X					TRANSFORMATIVE
6. Value-Chain Focus	DESIGN-MAKE		X				MARKET-DELIVER
7. Learning Focus	INDIVIDUAL	X					GROUP

FACILITATING FACTORS	Little evidence to support this factor		Some evidence to support this factor			Extensive evidence to support this factor	
	1	2	3	4	5	6	7
1. Scanning Imperative		X					
2. Performance Gap			X				
3. Concern for Measurement	X						
4. Organizational Curiosity			X		X		
5. Climate of Openness			X				
6. Continuous Education						X	
7. Operational Variety				X			
8. Multiple Advocates		X					
9. Involved Leadership					X		
10. Systems Perspective	X						

Unit Being Profiled _____

Names of Participants _____

Company and Phone Number _____

Date of Profile _____

Source: Darling and Hennessy, 1995.

Figure 6.6.   Learning Charter of the Harvard University Law Library

CHARTING A CORPORATE LEARNING STRATEGY

Learning Charter: Goals and Objectives

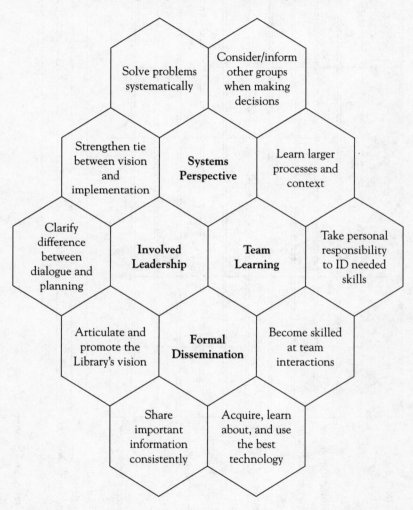

Source: Darling and Hennessy, 1995, p. 5. Used by permission of the publisher.

The cluster shown in Figure 6.6 was used as a basis for a rotating team of "organizational learning stewards" who will meet periodically to review progress on the initial commitments. It was decided that every six months the commitments will be exchanged for a new list based on progress made during that period.

These two cases illustrate the way learning profiles can be used to develop a learning strategy. In the following chapter we turn our attention to a detailed look at how to select elements for action and what the implications are in making different choices.

7

Improving Organizational Learning Capability

We now turn our attention to the task of selecting elements to build learning capability. How does an organization decide what areas to focus on? What are the implications of selecting different elements? As it is virtually impossible to focus on all seventeen elements at once, how does an organization decide where to concentrate? Each situation will have unique characteristics and opportunities, and each will present its own set of barriers to change, whether in general or with regard to specific actions.

One place to begin is to see how a team interprets its own learning profile. The following questions can prompt discussion:

1. Can team members explain any extreme data points or relationships between factors?

2. Are they surprised by any of the data points?

3. How does the profile of LOrs complement or conflict with those of other work groups or teams in the same organization or firm?

4. Which FFs were rated highest? Which were rated lowest? What is the implication of this pattern?

Another approach for selecting elements is to identify critical leverage points. Facilitating Factors are elements in the conceptual framework that promote learning. Teams may get better at their learning style by improving the status of their FFs while keeping their LOrs constant. To develop the learning capability of their teams or organizations, participants may analyze which FFs affect learning capability the most. As each learning system is unique, it is possible to use team members' ideas about the criticality of each FF. One way to do this is to create a plot diagram with "significance of factor" on the Y axis and "amount of evidence" on the X axis (see Figure 7.1). The latter can be taken from the learning profile(s); the former needs to be solicited from team members.

This exercise requires that participants rank the relative importance of the ten FFs. This ranking is plotted against the profile(s) of FFs. The ideal result would be an upwardly curving line or a straight line with a positive slope. (If data from multiple groups are plotted, there should be as many lines as groups.) Either result would suggest that the work group has strong capabilities in those FFs that count the most. If the shape of the plotted data deviates from the ideal line, it can point out those factors a team should work on for maximum effect.

Focus on Organizational Learning Cycle

Another approach to creating action plans to build learning capability is to focus on those elements that have an impact on particular phases of the learning cycle. In this chapter we discuss the three elements critical to all phases; in Chapter Eight we focus on the other fourteen elements in terms of their special significance at a respective phase. We present questions and guidelines for each of these elements. As we indicated in Chapter Six, ideas for learning improvement may come from a combination of elements that cut across the three phases.

The guidelines and questions represent only a fraction of what should be considered in making choices about the best way to improve organizational effectiveness through enhanced learning

Figure 7.1. Plot Diagram of Facilitating Factors by Evidence

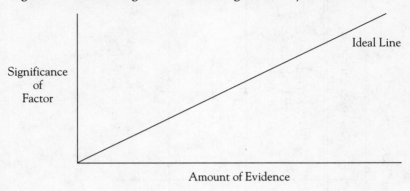

capability. We hope this is sufficient to point the way to actions that make a difference. We have not attempted to write a comprehensive book about change but rather to broaden and deepen your awareness of what is required to improve organizational learning. You will need to make your own choices about which elements to address. You will also need to draw from your own ideas, as well as ours, in dealing with the dynamic and complex setting with which you are involved.

We propose that you begin by selecting the phase of the learning cycle that seems most in question: Knowledge Acquisition, Knowledge Dissemination, or Knowledge Utilization. These phases were discussed in Chapter Two. In Figure 2.3 we first listed the Learning Orientations and Facilitating Factors that appear to be most relevant for improvement at each phase in the learning cycle. (Figure 7.2 contains the same information in a different format.) This does not mean that they are not relevant at the other phases, but that there is some extra gain to be had by looking at each in relation to the three phases. Note that we have identified two Facilitating Factors (Involved Leadership and Systems Perspective) and one Learning Orientation (Learning Focus) as essential to success in building capability at all three stages of the learning

Figure 7.2. Enhancing Learning Capabilities at Different Phases of the Learning Cycle

	Knowledge Acquisition	Knowledge Dissemination	Knowledge Utilization
Basic Variables Required at All Stages	Involved Leadership - Systems Perspective Learning Focus	Involved Leadership Systems Perspective Learning Focus	Involved Leadership Systems Perspective Learning Focus
Shift Learning Orientations	Knowledge Source Content-Process Focus	Knowledge Reserve Dissemination Mode	Learning Scope Value-Chain Focus
Improve Facilitating Factors	Scanning Imperative Performance Gap Concern for Measurement Organizational Curiosity	Climate of Openness Continuous Education	Multiple Advocates Operational Variety

Knowledge Acquisition: development or creation of insights, skills, or relationships

Knowledge Dissemination: dissemination to others of what has been acquired by some

Knowledge Utilization: assimilation of learning so that it is broadly available and can also be applied to new situations

cycle. Our data and the results of numerous studies at the MIT Center for Organizational Learning indicate that organizational units that are strong in these two Facilitating Factors and know how to choose a Learning Focus that is relevant to their structure, culture, and degree of interdependence generally have a better chance of learning.

Enhancing the Three Broadly Applicable Elements

Involved Leadership

As indicated in Chapter Four, this Facilitating Factor has to do with the extent to which leaders of an organizational unit are personally involved as learners in any effort to enhance learning.

Involvement is critical at all levels of the organization, not just the senior level. Involvement ranges from simply spending time with people to listen and learn what is going on, to active participation in implementing programs and actions to facilitate learning, to actual participation as a learner in educational and on-the-job interventions. It calls for face-to-face interaction with people and for the use of one's presence as an instrument of influence. It requires the leader to act as a model, hoping to get others excited about what matters and presenting an example of the behavior or attitude to be learned. This involvement is quite different from that of command and control, where leaders tend to see their interactions with people in terms of performance evaluation. Nor does it have anything to do with attempting to do anyone else's job because of problems in delegating or trusting others.

Many leaders, particularly senior management, may have some difficulty in adopting this style, for it goes against the more detached manner preached and taught to them for decades. With the advent of scientific management some fifty years ago, it became fashionable to exhort managers to direct most of their effort to planning and analysis and to stay hands-off at the operational level. The growth of managed work teams, in which the role of supervisors has changed dramatically, has encouraged this trend at lower levels of the organization. We now know that this aloofness is not suitable if learning is the objective. Among other things, it prevents leaders from going beyond the filtered information they often receive.

One of the problems in changing this state of affairs has to do with the discomfort many leaders feel about getting close to others. Also, if managers do not feel at home with the role of the learner they will find this hard to do. Involved Leadership can be enhanced through the following activities:

- Benchmarking with identified models at all levels both within and outside the organization

- Providing coaches who can help managers examine their assumptions and fears

- Attending leadership courses emphasizing self-analysis (the NTL Institute, Center for Creative Leadership, University of Chicago summer program in Aspen, Colorado, and the like)

- Asking managers to conduct small studies in which they interview and otherwise observe particular individuals or processes

- Including managers as actual participants in educational programs for those they supervise

Systems Perspective

Our data clearly indicate that most organizations score very low on this Facilitating Factor. Jay Forrester, the founder of MIT's renowned Systems Dynamics Group, found after many years of intense effort that this is one of the hardest skills to teach adults.

It goes against much of our training and experience, which tends to focus on limited ends or specialized knowledge. In most organizational settings people advance by becoming expert in a focused area and then find themselves working at levels where integration and broad perspective are required. They have little experience in this way of functioning.

Systems Perspective can be enhanced in several ways:

- Exposure to formal programs in systems dynamics

- Job rotation and other experiences that enable people to see other perspectives than the one they are most versed in

- Bringing diverse groups of stakeholders together to solve problems affecting the entire organization

- Revamping reward systems drastically so that coordinated effort is rewarded and suboptimization is reduced

- Hiring, training, and orienting managers at the corporate level before they are assigned to local work groups

These practices are very helpful in breaking down or opening up rigid boundaries that develop in organizations and pushing people toward assuming a larger perspective than they usually do in their day-to-day work. Most essential is to change reward systems to support optimization of the whole as opposed to optimization of individuals or local concerns. If the parts of an organization that must work together in a highly interdependent way are rewarded for narrow behavior, there is no incentive to work for the good of the whole. Rewards must be based on the integrated behavior of all of the parts if a Systems Perspective is to prevail. Rewards also need to be based in part on how well a work group analyzes the processes and structures of the system and is able to identify the consequences of its actions on other parts of the system.

Finally, we caution that enhancement of Systems Perspective is not just a matter of changing attitudes. It requires that managers be educated in the tools, strategies, and skills that are required to make systems work better. Indeed, it may be necessary to do this as a means of changing attitudes. Fortunately, we now have a well-developed body of knowledge and some very skilled experts who can be drawn upon for this purpose.

Learning Focus

There has been much emphasis on team learning in recent years. The argument is that organizational learning is improved greatly by having people learn collectively and by teaching skills in collaborative work. Our data show clearly that most organizations invest more in individual skill development than in the building of group skills. Intuitively it would seem that we need to shift more in the group direction. However, the strategic choice here is a complicated one. To begin with, the desire to enhance group learning should not be done at the expense of needed individual skill development. This is not an either-or issue but one of complementarity. We found that highly effective individual learning contributes heavily to organizational success. In fact there are settings where there is only a minimal need to work in a group. It is not clear how much would be gained by shifting to collective learning in these settings.

There is also a tendency to think of enhancing team learning through formal educational programs. This is certainly not the only way to educate; personnel assignment criteria can be amended to include group composition and the selection of team leaders who can model and teach these skills on the job. Studies at the MIT Center for Organizational Learning found that having work teams engage in joint analysis of their underlying assumptions and in building new mental models is a very useful approach to collaborative learning. Rather than relying totally on learning in a classroom, organizational members also learn together by tackling a common problem with the help of trained facilitators. A well-known international pharmaceutical firm has more than thirty multinational research teams, each with a group skills facilitator. Individual skill learning is handled through personal development methods or firmwide skill programs.

These considerations led us to ask several questions in deciding upon actions with regard to this element:

- Can we differentiate between needs for individual and team learning in a given setting?

- What are the actual needs for team learning in a situation? Simply advocating it does not tell us how much of what kinds of skills are needed.

- How can we balance investments in tuition reimbursement and educational leaves (usually individual learning), investment in group training of work teams and departments, and use of on-the-job facilitators or models for both individual and team learning?

We offer the following as actions that can enhance capability in either approach of this Learning Orientation.

Group Learning

- In forming work groups, task forces, and the like, selection of members should be based partly on how well they can teach and support each other.

- Conduct in-house educational efforts only with groups of people who must work closely with each other.

- Teach system dynamics through team analysis of actual, current problems.

- Teach group process analysis and group effectiveness behaviors.

Individual Learning

- Use career development programs in which each individual sets a personal learning goal each year.

- Encourage and support (with time and money) self-elected learning plans of all members of the organization.

- Establish local resource centers that organization members can use for self-guided learning.

- Enable individuals to do benchmarking around issues or processes that interest them.

The Power of the Three Dimensions

We have been discussing elements one by one. However, our experience indicates that there is a powerful synergy in combining them, and that lack of one of them diminishes the potency of effective behavior on the other two. For example, an organization with high Involved Leadership but poor Systems Perspective will hamper the development of its learning capability whether or not it prefers an individual or group Learning Focus. The reason is that the acquired learning will pertain only to a narrowly defined part of the organization. Executives at Motorola are convinced that the single thing that will leverage what they have accomplished to date is to enhance significantly a broad understanding and acceptance of a Systems Perspective.

Likewise, poor Involved Leadership will reduce the gain to be had from either an individual or group Learning Focus. In this situation others may learn a great deal, but without learning on the part of the leadership use of this knowledge is limited.

In studies of firms that appear to do a good job in developing learning capability, we can see how important these elements are—even if they are not consciously recognized. A review of published reports on companies such as GE, Oticon (a Danish company), Semco (a Brazilian company), ABB, and WalMart shows a pattern in which all three play an important part. Another example for which we have a great deal of data is Motorola. Although a study of this firm indicates concern with numerous elements, the three described in this chapter have been critical to enhancement of its learning capability. A discussion of Motorola follows.

With this chapter as a starting point we can now discuss actions related to each phase of the organizational learning cycle. The next chapter focuses on the elements in our framework that best develop learning capability at a particular phase.

Case Study: Motorola—A Firm in Search of Learning

We discuss organizational learning at Motorola not because it is the best learning organization we can identify but because it provided us with particularly rich insights. Motorola did not start out to become a learning organization. It has a history of being able to make significant changes in its product lines, spurred on by the deeply entrenched notion of "renewal" created by its founder many years ago. Since 1978 it has embarked on a large number of initiatives to improve learning, beginning with its now-renowned success in total quality management. These efforts were not driven by a picture of our model but by an intuitive understanding that many of our elements were important. Perhaps more important, they were bolstered by trial-and-error learning experiments that began with the CEO's curiosity and desire to learn.

Analysis of Motorola indicates that ten of our seventeen elements played an important part in its learning improvement efforts. These are indicated here, together with an elaboration of how they played out.

Three Learning Orientations: Value-Chain Focus (a desire to become better at the market-and-deliver end of this Learning Orientation),

Learning Focus (a desire to improve group skills and team learning), and Dissemination Mode (a desire to make knowledge more available through formal methods)

Seven Facilitating Factors: Scanning Imperative, Performance Gap, Concern for Measurement, Continuous Education, Multiple Advocates, Involved Leadership, and Systems Perspective

Motorola is one of the world's leading providers of electronic equipment, systems, and services and is among the United States' fifty largest industrial companies. Its founder, Paul Galvin, believed in a concept of renewal that led to significant redefinition of products and businesses throughout its history. Starting with a "battery eliminator," the firm moved on to car and home radios, police department systems, military radios (walkie-talkies), semiconductors, paging systems, cellular telephones, and more. Motorola is a dominant force in its markets and, as the first winner of the Malcolm Baldrige National Quality Award given in the United States since 1988, is perceived as a leader in total quality programs.

Our study at Motorola began with observations over several months of two senior management teams, each composed of twenty to twenty-five executives from all parts of the corporation. Each group focuses on a critical real-time problem defined by the CEO and COO to whom the groups report. Our objective was to see how these groups function as action learning systems and to study how learning developed during the history of the quality program and related activities since 1979. In addition to group observations, individual interviews were held with about 30 percent of the members and an additional twenty people, and we visited the paging products operation in the United States.

Changes That Came from Organizational Learning

In meetings of both executive groups, frequent references to the history of Motorola's quality initiative were made; members wondered how they can apply what was learned in the past to the strategic initiatives of today. As the groups carried out their task, they made repeated referrals to this learning, some of which was summarized in papers prepared by members of the teams. With regard to Motorola's fourteen-year quality program, a learning process emerged in several stages. It began with a vague but growing fear of competition, mainly from the Japanese, that led Motorola's CEO to become aware of quality problems. An initial training program and the appointment of quality consultants did little to alter product quality. Through intensive benchmarking the company developed a more precise definition of its quality goals, programs, and metrics (for example, "from Three Sigma to Six Sigma"). These goals were broadened to encompass suppliers, customers, and learning consortiums, and rewards and recognition programs were used to reinforce the application and extension of learning.

Several changes were made on the basis of what was learned during this process. First, a customer focus emerged. The corporate intelligence group was reorganized to become a center for benchmarking capability and to be more available for strategic inputs. Benchmarking became highly acceptable and used widely, as in the two initiatives observed in this study.

Second, there was widespread recognition that organization-wide quality at all levels of the firm could not be achieved without a huge investment in education. Moreover, it was recognized that team functioning had to be improved through team learning. As a result, several large-scale initiatives were undertaken. One was the development of a range of formal programs that became institutionalized throughout the company. Another was the formation of quality teams that worked together and made presentations at an annual quality meeting and competition. (In 1993, 3,000 quality teams participated in this event.) Yet another was to educate hundreds of managers in systems thinking.

Third, the very ways in which the executive groups were formed is worthy of mention. These groups were designed to overcome barriers among different divisions who tended not to learn from each other because of their internal product focus and resource competitiveness. The two strategic groups we observed built their process on what was learned from the quality initiative. For example, they spent a significant amount of time developing documentation and dissemination methods to improve knowledge sharing across the firm. They also realized that the usual Motorola focus on product-oriented learning would have to be modified to allow for more learning about process. With the help of specialists in planning, scanning, measurement, and educational design, the groups created new management and learning processes for an improved Systems Perspective.

Fourth, a charter for one of the senior executive groups emerged from a desire to improve organizational effectiveness on the market-and-deliver end of the value chain. This was seen as a needed balance to the enormous effort devoted to the design-and-make end of the value chain. The charter asked the executives to undertake, as a learning and implementation task, the development of a new and better integrated approach to marketing in a particular geographic region. The executives defined this mission as a long-term project and committed themselves to work on it for several years.

How Learning Occurs

Much of the learning at higher management levels at Motorola emerges through the involvement of staff in action learning, where actual problems form the basis of education design. This is supported by a wide array of knowledge dissemination programs available to staff on both a voluntary and required basis. Another vehicle for learning is the development and participation of joint ventures with other firms so that knowledge acquisition, dissemination, and utilization are made faster and more robust through the sharing of diverse resources. There is still heavy reliance on local and individual learning, but more attention is devoted to formal dissemination. (We were given over fifty documents developed for sharing knowledge inside and outside the firm.)

With regard to the quality initiative, several factors helped enormously:

1. The quality program leaped ahead when multiple champions were developed. The CEO spearheaded the initial effort, but not until "champions" were enlisted at all levels and parts of the firm did knowledge acquisition and sharing become powerful forces.

2. Benchmarking was seen as an essential step in the learning process.

3. The effort at metric definition had a big payoff. Managers were given an opportunity to develop their own metrics using the experience as learning.

4. The language used in defining and promoting an initiative can make a big difference. Learning came from "naming the change" and using new metaphors and symbols, such as "Six Sigma."

5. There was a broad use of education to support the quality effort. It was assumed that high quality standards cannot be achieved with an uneducated workforce.

Several other factors contributed to learning at Motorola. First is an historic drive to stay ahead of the competition, which has permeated the firm since its founding. Fear of becoming a loser was a strong motivating factor. Second, this is a company that has reinvented itself several times in its history and, at least in the realm of products, has responded energetically to new challenges. Third, for a period of about thirty years CEO Bob Galvin played a pivotal role in being curious about the outside world and in personally driving learning investments. He himself was a student in the first stages of the quality endeavor and modeled concern for process improvements and quality systems in his meetings with executives, making it the first item on the agenda in operations review sessions. Fourth, interest in internal education efforts was revitalized, leading to the creation of

Motorola University. This made a strong statement internally and externally that the company would make a substantial investment in education. As of 1996, Motorola spent 5 percent of its revenues on education of all kinds.

The preceding narrative is a summary of some of Motorola's learning history since 1978. It demonstrates the relevance of our approach and how organizational learning can be understood by focusing on specific Learning Orientations and Facilitating Factors. Motorola built learning capability by enhancing its competence in ten of the seventeen elements in our framework.

8

Enhancing Effectiveness at Each Phase of the Learning Cycle

We now turn our attention to choosing actions concerning the elements that are most relevant to each of the three phases of the learning cycle. As with the discussion in Chapter Seven, we offer guidelines and hope that you will be stimulated to develop concrete action plans that include your own ideas.

Choices Related to Knowledge Acquisition

Knowledge Acquisition has to do with the development of concepts and methods. It addresses the issue of how to identify the insights, skills, and relationships that can lead to improved organizational performance and to increased interest in ongoing learning. This area may be selected for improvement if analysis of current functioning indicates some serious gaps or weaknesses in the creation or development of appropriate knowledge. Six elements—two Learning Orientations (Knowledge Source and Content-Process Focus) and four Facilitating Factors (Scanning Imperative, Performance Gap, Concern for Measurement, and Organizational Curiosity)—are relevant to improvement of Knowledge Acquisition and are discussed in detail.

Learning Orientations Related to Knowledge Acquisition

Two Learning Orientations have particular impact on Knowledge Acquisition: Knowledge Source and Content-Process Focus. These have to do with learning investment decisions: What shall we build as core competences? What shall we buy or adapt from the knowledge of others? What are the minimum knowledge bases required to achieve our mission?

The strategic dilemma is easy to pose but difficult to manage in any organizational unit, whether it be a small work group or the entire firm. There are few guidelines for making decisions here; these are judgment calls made in relation to the competence that an organization has established. All firms develop an "investment bank" over time. At any given time the ability of an organization to change in a fundamental way must be weighed against the ease and cost of building on what presently exists. Rather than provide definitive answers, we offer a list of questions to consider in managing this dilemma:

- How explicit is an organization's choice to invest in internal Knowledge Acquisition versus investing in adaptation of external knowledge?

- What is an appropriate investment in internal research and development?

- What is an appropriate investment in buying knowledge from others?

- To what extent can we capitalize on process capabilities that might apply to several products?

- To what extent can we leverage our content-oriented capabilities to stay ahead of competition with enhanced product features?

- If we are heavily invested at one end or the other of these two Learning Orientations, is this adequate or should we seek a greater balance in one or both?

Chapter Three contains examples of companies that have been successful at both approaches in these LOrs. Most pharmaceutical firms prefer to emphasize internal knowledge sources and spend significant amounts of money on internal R&D. However, American Home Products is an extremely successful company as a result of its emphasis on taking the research of others and leveraging it through powerful marketing and distribution systems. Many other examples can be provided. The important point is that an organization needs to determine where it is on the continuum and decide whether it is able to exploit this preference further or whether a shift to another position would better capitalize on its skills and its culture.

To move from one side to another along an LOr continuum, here are some available actions.

Knowledge Source

To move from internal to external source:

- Study or benchmark other organizations that have been successful.

- Seek out organizations that have developed some of the knowledge you desire and negotiate for use of this knowledge.

- Support "gatekeepers," those organization members who reach outside the organization and try to bring knowledge inside.

- Determine what strengths you have that can be added to outside knowledge to create an enhanced product or service.

- Increase travel budget for staff to attend national and international conferences.

To move from external to internal source:

- Determine areas in which increased R&D seems promising.

- Maximize return on investment from "cash cows" so that funds are available to support long-term development efforts.

- Hire some outside people with successful histories of internal knowledge development; they can serve as role models of a new way of working.

Content-Process Focus

To move from content to process focus:

- Benchmark with organizations who have a strong process orientation (for example, Canon, Federal Express).

- Offer incentives for process improvements as well as for productivity gain.

- Engage in Business Process Reengineering, TQM programs, or both.

- Introduce periodic group review of progress on projects and programs.

To move from process to content focus:

- Study ways to improve product or service features.

- Engage industrial designers to enhance your product image.

- Eliminate or shorten the amount of time spent in analysis of process improvements.

- Use focus groups to obtain ideas and reactions for product development.

Facilitating Factors Related to Knowledge Acquisition

Four elements have special impact on Knowledge Acquisition: Scanning Imperative, Performance Gap, Concern for Measurement, and Organizational Curiosity. Each of these has to do with the ability to take in data, to be curious about our world, and to be interested in discovering new ways of doing things. In a sense, this is the stance of an experimental scientist; those who want to improve organizational learning must adopt this posture to some extent. We believe that management development efforts need to be shifted to include the skills of observation, data gathering, and risk taking to support people in opening up to ways of improving acquisition of knowledge. It will also be necessary to alter reward systems to recognize staff for trying new things as part of ongoing learning efforts. As long as immediate results and stable operational control are the total basis for rewards, there will be little incentive to develop the needed skills or to make pilot investigations or experiments.

As with the discussion concerning Learning Orientations, we offer some key questions to consider and possible actions to take in improving Knowledge Acquisition.

Scanning Imperative

If more scanning is better, who do we select to perform enhanced scanning? What should we look at? All information is not equal and some can be of negative consequence. What methods should we use? Here are specific actions to consider:

- Develop a list of critical success factors and how external events may impinge on them.

- Form an intelligence-gathering group at the business unit level.

- Increase participation in industry, economic, and professional associations.

- Arrange for people who typically work inside the organization to make visits to customers and suppliers.

- Ask field (sales, service, distribution) personnel to gather select information beyond the immediate concerns of their work.

Performance Gap

How can we use benchmarking to increase the ability of managers to accept disconfirming feedback? What is the best way to stop managers from projecting blame onto others for poor performance? How can we teach managers to create visions that motivate people to look at new paradigms or reach for new goals? Here are specific actions to consider:

- Arrange for group leaders to benchmark with organizations deemed world-class in a particular area.

- Provide special incentives for people to examine performance problems.

- Provide a consultant to assist in examination of performance gaps, particularly to focus the group on looking at the role it plays.

- Involve people at all levels in creating visions of a more desirable future state.

Concern for Measurement

How do we convince managers of the importance of measurements related to learning, as opposed to those that indicate the financial status of the business? What should be measured? Who should develop the measures? Here are specific actions to consider:

- Conduct seminars in the "new accounting" model, such as "Kaplan's Balanced Scorecard" (Kaplan and Norton, 1992).

- Distribute widely reports discussing the measurements in TQM programs.

- Include up-front work on development of metrics in all new initiatives, using specialists only in support of the line people for whom this will be a learning experience.

- Teach people the rudiments of statistical measurement of behavior and attitudes.

Organizational Curiosity

How can we get people interested in at least looking at new ideas or methods? Is it possible to lighten up our organizational climate and become more playful and imaginative? How can we design experiments for "small wins" so that each tryout does not bet the entire organization? Here are specific actions to consider:

- Engage in creativity training.

- Institutionalize brainstorming as an essential aspect of all problem solving.

- Provide some kind of nonfinancial recognition for people who try something that does not work but from which learning is derived.

- Try out new things in parallel systems so that the current approach is maintained while the experiment is being conducted.

- Establish rituals to celebrate milestones, project completions, and the like.

Choices Related to Knowledge Dissemination

If analysis of the organizational unit indicates that useful knowledge is acquired reasonably well but is not readily available to significant others, the unit may decide to work on the knowledge dissemination phase of the learning cycle. Many of the organizations from which we obtained data tell us that dissemination is a much bigger problem than acquisition. So much knowledge is being gathered and organization members are increasingly so dispersed that effective dissemination appears to be an overwhelming task. Who needs to know what and what needs to be shared as a matter of routine have become major issues in this age of knowledge. The process actually begins with how knowledge is documented, codified, and elaborated.

Four elements are critical to this area of intervention, two Learning Orientations (Knowledge Reserve and Dissemination Mode) and two Facilitating Factors (Climate of Openness and Continuous Education).

Learning Orientations Related to Knowledge Reserve and Dissemination Mode

The first step in building learning capability in Knowledge Reserve is to engage in a dialogue about how the organization defines knowledge and what knowledge is considered important for doing the unit's work. Most organizations tend to take such definitions for granted and are not accustomed to examining different ways of defining knowledge. Yet this is an essential step before considering how to document what is considered important. After that the organization is ready to look at how it documents knowledge. If this reflection suggests the need for movement to a more public (as opposed to personal) orientation, then creation of on-line databases, critical incident and case reports, and libraries can be created as effective documentation methods. Nonaka (1991) suggests another approach in which groups of people work with, watch, and interview experts about their process and then document what they have learned.

Most organizations devote considerable effort to dissemination of what they consider to be important and useful knowledge, yet they are generally frustrated in achieving the results they desire. One of the reasons is that systems are developed from the point of view of upper management or specialists rather than being generated by users, who may have very different ideas about what is important. Another is the overload of information being distributed in many places, such that few things truly stand out as being critical.

Whatever the reason, characteristic preferences in Dissemination Mode do develop. Those who prefer formal modes may control the channels of distribution, but at least things are codified, organized, and shared in a disciplined way. These proponents may not recognize the power of informal means. Thus if organizations structure themselves so that it is difficult for members to exchange information through methods they control (such as "down-time" conversations, e-mail networks, and the like), there is a danger that a lot of knowledge that is not easily codified will be lost or made available only to a few people. Those who prefer the informal mode often find ways to get around this problem. In one very successful consulting firm, technical specialists and middle-level managers developed their own e-mail networks and telephone conferences to expand on and exchange knowledge. There is a problem with this approach if the outcomes of these interactions are not formally disseminated to a larger audience within the firm. In this instance, there are many comments by people not "in the loop" to the effect that they do not know what is going on or have a hard time getting their hands on the knowledge generated by a network.

Here are some important questions to ask:

- If we prefer a personal mode, how is knowledge captured? Is important knowledge sometimes unavailable because individuals possessing it are not available for one reason or another?

- If we are highly public in Knowledge Reserve, does this stifle individual creativity or fail to capture what Polyani called "tacit knowledge"?

- Informal and formal Dissemination Modes require different managerial skills. What is the fit between our preferred mode and our competence model for managers?

- How can we integrate the best of both formal and informal dissemination? How would we shift our learning investments to accomplish this?

Here are some action steps to consider.
To move from personal to public Knowledge Reserve:

- Develop systems for capturing, codifying, and aggregating experience of individuals and groups.

- Routinely interview experts about their processes so that they can articulate publicly what is often not consciously known or spoken.

- Ensure that all critical work processes are well documented on a current basis.

- Prepare project reports that are part of a shared repository.

- Improve and extend policy and procedure manuals.

- Conduct exit interviews with personnel who are leaving the organization to capture their expert knowledge.

- Form communities of practice for staff to build shared, tacit knowledge.

- Support events that embed knowledge in corporate culture.

To move from public to personal Knowledge Reserve:

- Encourage individuals to engage in professional reflection.

- Encourage individuals to maintain a learning journal in which they capture their personal learning.

- Support the development of personal databases.

- Provide many varied avenues for learning but allow individuals to choose those that appeal to them.

- Recognize the value of individual subjective experience as well as "hard data."

To move from informal to formal Dissemination Mode:

- Develop communication systems that are available to many people (e-mail, Lotus Notes, and the like).

- Increase use of formal education modes as a means of spreading important knowledge.

- Make external reports and publications widely available.

- Target mixed combinations of people (for example, cross-functional teams) to receive information they might not receive otherwise.

To move from formal to informal Dissemination Mode:

- Make greater use of apprenticeship models of learning.

- Support the development of networks initiated by individuals.

- Enable occupational groups to engage in informal dialog (communities of practice).

- Provide libraries and databases from which people can pick and choose.

- Encourage everyone to have a mentor.

Facilitating Factors Related to Climate of Openness and Continuous Education

Two Facilitating Factors are especially relevant to Knowledge Dissemination: Climate of Openness and Continuous Education. Openness is the extent to which the existence of boundaries influences the exchange of knowledge and experience. It deals with issues of trust, flexibility in command and control, and assumptions about how on-the-job learning occurs. Many factors converge to create the level of openness in an organization.

History has a great influence over today's attempts to enhance openness. One cannot simply say that we need to trust each other more when many years of low trust have left their mark. The worst way to address the problem is to mount a formal campaign that confronts senior management with an ideological position implying that the current position is bad and needs to be changed. The best way is simply to do small day-to-day things that lead to small changes. Over time, the small steps will aggregate and, in effect, a new ideology will be created. By small steps we mean such things as inviting subordinates who have worked on a report to be part of the presentation group or to witness the presentation. This approach, which has been called "legitimate peripheral participation," is a powerful way of enhancing learning.

For improving trust, the newly popular large-scale interventions show much promise. Bringing large numbers of stakeholders together to share and work on common problems reduces the degree of projection that keeps past attitudes and rumors alive. These interventions also address organizational assumptions and practices concerning privacy of information.

Some words about Continuous Education are in order. At first it appears that this Facilitating Factor is most relevant to Knowledge Acquisition rather than to Knowledge Dissemination. There is some truth to this, but we believe that Continuous Education affords one of the best opportunities for disseminating knowledge, particularly when group formats are employed. By group format we mean more than classroom interventions; we include any situation where organization members join together, such as task forces and networks. These formats encourage sharing and joint problem solving, which are wonderful opportunities for learning if they are viewed as more than simply doing a job. When so viewed, it is a relatively easy step to ask people to discuss what they have learned from their work on a joint endeavor.

The gain from Continuous Education is also enhanced by giving organization members more say in selecting developmental experiences both within and outside the organization. Learning is always greater when there is a high degree of ownership by the learner.

Here are some critical questions to consider:

- Where and when did our assumptions about the ideal working climate come from? Are these assumptions valid today?

- How do our assumptions about who participates in what, and who receives various sources of information, enhance or inhibit learning?

- Can we locate respected role models who can be enlisted in the task of learning to be more open and inviting?

- If we discarded all the educational interventions we use (internally and externally) and designed a new approach to continuous education, what would we do differently?

- How can we maximize group learning in on-the-job experiences?

Here are some specific actions to consider.
To encourage Climate of Openness:

- Conduct frequent, casual, informal discussions between unit leaders and others.

- Make otherwise reserved information available on a broad basis.

- Engage in conflict resolution interventions with groups that do not relate well to each other.

- Encourage rather than disparage expressions of emotion and disagreement.

- Conduct meetings with the largest number of relevant people whom it is practical to bring together (use open space or search conference techniques).

- Teach people the value of legitimate peripheral participation, the practice of inviting select people to meetings and other events for the purpose of exposing them to a broader perspective.

To encourage Continuous Education:

- Establish a target of a percentage of gross revenues to be used for education.

- Create "learning vouchers" that can be used by individuals for education, including courses, attendance at conferences, and the like.

- Encourage senior members of the organizational unit to attend educational events and make their participation widely visible.

- Design task forces and special initiatives so that they contain structures and processes for learning as well as for producing results.

- Conduct developmental performance reviews that include mutually agreed upon learning goals for individuals.

Choices Related to Knowledge Utilization

The area of Knowledge Utilization represents the ultimate payoff for learning yet is the least understood of the three stages of the learning process. Managers tell us that this is the area they most need to improve. They say that they have a reasonably good grasp of what it takes to be effective in Knowledge Acquisition and Knowledge Dissemination, but that only a small portion of the knowledge they acquire and disseminate becomes broadly used or applied in new situations.

For true assimilation of knowledge to take place, people must be able to embrace a new mental model and make their own meaning out of their experience in approaching something new. Two things that help but are often overlooked in organizational life are the ability of the learner to ask questions about what is not clear and a requirement that the learner be able to articulate what has been learned—perhaps even be asked to teach it to others. The first of these behaviors is inhibited by the need to save face in a world that rewards certainty. The second is often seen as too time-consuming or as an unnecessary delay in turning attention to something else.

In addition to the primary elements of Involved Leadership, Systems Perspective, and Learning Focus, we see four elements as being of special importance to improving Knowledge Utilization: two Learning Orientations—Learning Scope and Value-Chain Focus—and two Facilitating Factors—Operational Variety and Multiple Advocates.

Learning Orientations Related to Knowledge Utilization

Knowledge Utilization represents the ultimate payoff in learning. It has to do with knowledge related to stability and change, and how well knowledge has been assimilated and made available for new learning. Two Learning Orientations are highly relevant for the improvement of Knowledge Utilization: Learning Scope and Value-Chain Focus.

Here are some critical questions to ask about these matters:

- Where are we on the stability-change cycle? Do we need to improve our learning curve for established ways or do we need to consider large-scale change?

- How ready are we to undertake transformative learning? What needs to be done to increase this readiness?

- If we are highly capable at the design-and-make end but less capable at the market-and-deliver end, should we attempt to change things through internal development or would we do better to develop external alliances?

- If we develop an alliance, how do we get our partner's knowledge to flow our way? How dependent upon the partner can we afford to be without putting ourselves in a highly vulnerable position?

- How much should we invest in improving what we do well, and how much should we invest in less-developed competences?

Learning Scope

Learning Scope is concerned with a preference for either incremental or transformative learning. An incremental focus adds to knowledge consistent with an existing set of values or paradigm.

Transformative learning seeks to develop a new model based on questioning the assumptions or reframing the current paradigm. Though this orientation has a strong influence on Knowledge Acquisition, we have chosen to place it under Knowledge Utilization in order to highlight a critical, often misunderstood phenomenon: *Knowledge Utilization efforts often stumble because of failure to distinguish whether the aim is to improve capabilities incrementally or to build a new basis for actionable knowledge (transformation)*. Each mode requires a different approach to implementation and each can be useful at different times. To enhance what is already accepted and internalized, rational thinking and intellectual persuasion may suffice. There are no certainties about what will work, but tried and true methods are readily available. To build a new base for actionable knowledge often requires emotional appeals and less structured approaches.

Moving from Incremental to Transformative Learning Scope   Enhancing transformative learning requires a powerful vision of the new, supported by emotional appeals and even some coercion. The goal is nothing less than to achieve a significant culture change. For this purpose it is frequently necessary to bring in the fresh perspectives of outsiders or nontraditional insiders to model a new way of being. Nevis, Lancourt, and Vassallo (1996) developed a seven-point strategy for transformative change and argue that these seven leverage points need to be used more or less simultaneously for high impact. The seven "modes of attack" are these:

1. Persuasive communication: enabling people to envision a different future

2. Participation: creating a shared reality through joint endeavor

3. Expectancy: using the power of self-fulfilling prophecy

4. Role modeling: showing how it's done

5. Structural rearrangement: shaping the work environment

6. Extrinsic rewards: reinforcing transformative behaviors

7. Coercion: using it legitimately

The Nevis-Lancourt-Vassallo model also takes into account that transformation usually goes through a series of stages in which some of these methods are utilized first and the others are applied later. In addition, they call attention to the importance of managing the multiple realities that exist in organizations, the many cultural sub-sets that determine the various ways in which any organizational situation is perceived. Figure 8.1 summarizes their conceptualization of the transformative process.

Note that the last three phases of transformational change roughly follow the stages of learning, with the first phases essentially

Figure 8.1.   A Three-Dimensional Model of Transformational Change

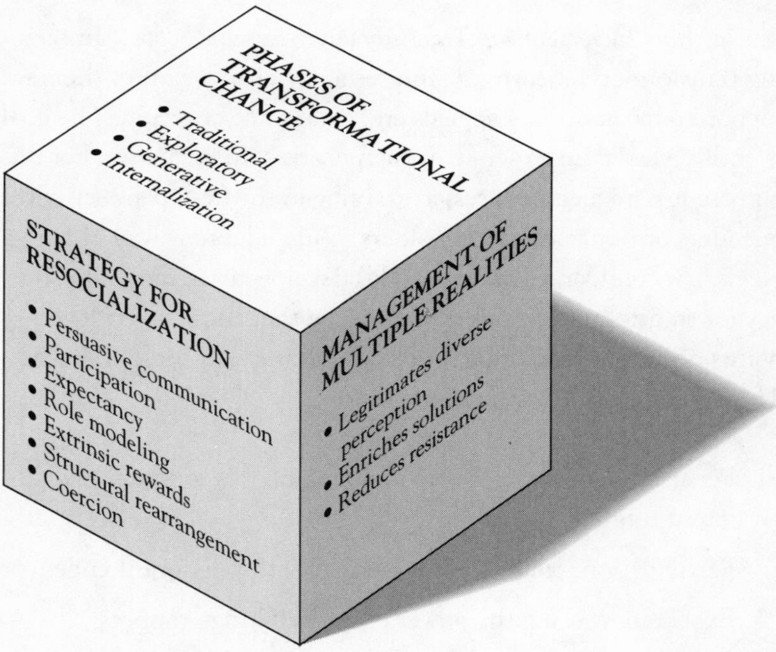

Source: Nevis, Lancourt, and Vassallo, 1996, p. 34. Used by permission of Jossey-Bass Inc., Publishers.

representing a prelearning mode. The exploratory phase is akin to Knowledge Acquisition, in which it is recognized that new or expanded knowledge is required and resources are committed to bring this about. The generative phase, which emphasizes open communication and increased participation by organization members, resembles our Facilitating Factors of Climate of Openness and Continuous Education. The internalization phase deals with the assimilation and broad use of what has been learned. This is similar to what we call Knowledge Utilization.

The implementation of transformational change is much too complex for a brief discussion at this point. In addition to Nevis, Lancourt, and Vassallo there are many books on the topic. However, we want to highlight two kinds of actions that are critical.

- *Use of new role models.* Using those who can readily exhibit the stance or the new behavior desired frequently means bringing in new people from outside the organization. In addition to providing visible evidence that a new paradigm can be actualized, this also sends a message that seemingly tight boundaries will now be treated more like permeable membranes. We are quite familiar with two situations in which visionary CEOs attempted to change the nature of their business through reassigning current members of the organization to the task of transformation and failed largely because there were no people available who could demonstrate the attitudes, skills, and behaviors required by the new model. By the time this was recognized, the firms had lost so much money that their boards of directors canceled the program.
- *Shifting rewards to new behaviors.* Development of new behavior-reward contingencies is often overlooked or mismanaged, as organizations continue to use incremental learning reward systems that are not properly applicable here. Table 8.1 compares rewards for incremental learning with those that are applicable to transformative learning.

Note that several of the desired behaviors and corresponding appropriate rewards for incremental learning provide incentives

Table 8.1.   Behavior-Reward Relationships in Incremental and Transformational Change Efforts

Change Objective	Desired Behaviors	Appropriate Rewards
Incremental (old reality)	Predictability of output; stability	Merit and longevity; salary increase; praise from work group manager
	Controlling behavior of others	Punishment systems
	Increased productivity	Increases related to units produced
	Limited work focus	Individual rewards; subunit profit center incentives
	Functional expertise	Educational opportunities such as conferences and schooling related to specific skills
	Short-term targets	Grant reward soon after the behavior
Transformational (new reality)	Flexibility; responsiveness	Reward process improvements; reward customer service activities
	Working under conditions of uncertainty, ambiguity, and transition	Reassurance of job security
	Experimental behavior	Reward tryouts and pilot projects using various recognition awards
	Broad skill acquisition	Knowledge-based pay system; educational opportunities that stretch
	Responsibility; independent decision making	Involvement in target setting and in more challenging work
	Coordinated collaborative work effort	Group incentives; multiple unit profit center incentives; companywide profit sharing

Table 8.1.   Behavior-Reward Relationships in Incremental and Transformational Change Efforts *(continued)*.

Change Objective	Desired Behaviors	Appropriate Rewards
Transformational	Developing and coaching others	Incentive rewards related to the performance of others
	Long-term results	Reward knowledge-generating activities; rewards based on performance over time

Source: Nevis, Lancourt, and Vassallo, 1996, p. 201. Used by permission of Jossey-Bass Inc., Publishers.

to improve skill and knowledge are currently being done. The behavior-reward sequences for transformation provide incentives for learning how to do something different. Both reward learning; they just focus on different aspects of it. This difference is often overlooked by drivers of change, who confuse production outcomes with learning outcomes and simply borrow incremental reward relationships for transformational use. The organizational change literature is full of examples where change failed because of mistaken behavior-reward contingencies.

Moving from Transformative to Incremental Learning Scope   Some organizations, particularly entrepreneur-driven start-ups, are very good at the transformative mode. In a sense, their reason for coming into being is related to a perceived new paradigm for doing business. In these instances the problem is often one of continuous change that does not allow time and space for incremental learning to take place or for stable performance to manifest itself. There is also much less attention paid to the development of systems that support orderly progress on a learning curve for specific activities and overall effectiveness. This often results in an unstable situation where the organization learns how to adjust to uncertainty and turmoil but not how to remain in a state of equilibrium long enough to gather experience with one way of doing something so that other kinds of useful learning are assimilated.

There is also a tendency to disparage the incremental level because it is not glamorous or because well-known firms got into trouble when they did not transform themselves quickly enough in fast-changing markets. In the 1970s American automobile companies experienced this difficulty, trying to apply an incremental approach when a transformative one was needed. Ironically, these firms had also let their incremental learning slip by, taking for granted the everyday "nuts and bolts" of manufacturing and running into severe quality problems. Although the success of the ensuing TQM movement required some transformative thinking, it was highly effective incremental learning that made it possible once a new paradigm was accepted. Thus both approaches are important at different times.

Here are some ways of enhancing the incremental Learning Scope:

- Introduce educational programs for increasing specific basic skills.

- Improve operating systems at all stages of the value chain.

- Implement changes in an orderly, unhurried manner.

- Reengineer processes so as to achieve continuous improvement.

- Develop daily feedback systems for everyday operating steps.

Value-Chain Focus

The case with Value-Chain Focus is interesting. This Learning Orientation influences Knowledge Acquisition and Dissemination, and it has special importance for Knowledge Utilization for several reasons. One is that a preferred orientation sends a powerful message to the entire organization as to where it will "place its stake in the ground." Everyone knows what counts the most, what will be most rewarded, and hence what learning must be assimilated at a deep level. Those parts of the organization that are less valued tend to accept this state of affairs even though it makes them somewhat marginal. A second reason is that the sheer aggregation of learning investments in this area creates a substantial critical mass of shared learning that can be enhanced or generalized to new problems that arise in the area.

A decision to shift to another position on the value-chain continuum invites a transformative strategy of large proportions. For this reason many firms decide to reinforce their preferred position and to develop alliances with other groups that have achieved greater knowledge in other areas of the value chain. As technological sophistication and worldwide competition have grown, more and more firms are examining this issue on an ongoing basis. At issue is establishing a clear picture of the organization's core competences and determining how to build on them instead of developing others.

Here are some ways to move from the design-and-make end of the value chain to the market-and-deliver end:

- Identify leading market-deliver organizations (in and out of your industry) and benchmark with them.

- Develop an alliance with a world-class marketing organization, taking advantage of its sales, service, and distribution expertise.

- Recruit market-deliver experts from outside the organization.

- Conduct an intensive educational effort to raise consciousness and develop skills in this area (marketing, selling, customer service, and the like).

- Have design-make managers make frequent visits to customers.

- Rotate people into jobs at the market-and-deliver side of the value chain.

Here are some ways to move from the market-and-deliver end of the value chain to the design-and-make end:

- Identify leading design-make organizations (in and out of your industry) and benchmark with them.

- Develop an alliance with a world-class engineering or manufacturing group or both.

- Recruit design-and-make experts from outside the organization.

- Conduct an intensive educational effort to raise consciousness and develop skills in this area (process engineering, TQM, and the like).

- Rotate people into jobs at the design-make side of the value chain.

- Increase budgets for R&D.

Facilitating Factors Related to Knowledge Utilization

Two elements are relevant here, Operational Variety and Multiple Advocates. Both of these Facilitating Factors make it possible for significant numbers of people to be involved in learning and in demonstrating that there are many ways to accomplish something. By working in different ways, we see variety and diversity as a way of internalizing the value of multiple approaches. In effect, the organization puts a stamp of approval on a pluralistic way of being.

It is not necessary that people imitate or adapt what they see; it is enough that they become interested in it and that they remain open to the validity of different approaches. This tolerance for ways other than one's own serves as a reinforcement for others to continue how they are working. Any way of being or working supports Knowledge Utilization by those demonstrating it, as they are supported to become more proficient in utilizing the knowledge acquired. It also provides alternative competences, any one of which may be available if needed to solve new problems that evolve. One of the best examples of this was found in MIC's Fixed Income Group, the case described in Chapter Four. In this highly successful firm, fund managers used three different methods for making investment decisions. This made visible to all that "more than one road leads to Rome." Advocates of any one of these positions may have looked down on the other approaches, but the fact is that this organization was building competence in three methods.

There is a great deal of resistance in the organizational world to having multiple policies or practices. This is one of the reasons GM established Saturn as an independent company. Saturn could go its own way without experiencing pressure to conform to the "GM way." It is now possible, due to the success (learning achievements) of Saturn, for GM to see how certain aspects might be tried by the parent organization.

Operational Variety is thus an important aspect of Knowledge Acquisition. However, we place it in the Knowledge Utilization category because any organization that supports it sends a very powerful message that people may utilize methods that appeal to them. This allows for a learning curve and reinforces practices until they become ingrained. Moreover, to allow Operational Variety is to eliminate much of the resistance that is experienced when people are forced to conform to any single way rather than allowed to achieve given outcomes in their own way.

The factor of Multiple Advocates has an impact because it allows many people to propose or support learning initiatives. This helps create a learning atmosphere that provides for more lasting effects in utilizing knowledge. Learning becomes the task of people at all levels. The work of Tom Allen (1971) and others shows us that advocates need not be drawn only from the ranks of senior management; in many cases highly respected people at lower levels carry enormous weight as advocates and frequently influence upper management to look at new ways of doing things. Anyone can be a "champion," and the more the better. In fact, many change efforts have failed because only a few people were driving the effort.

If this perspective makes sense, it follows that learning is supported by enrolling numerous people in the effort before attempting a rollout to large groups or the entire organization. This creates an energized coalition that educates itself, assimilates the skill or attitude, and then acts as teacher to others. This has an impact on Operational Variety in that the advocates soon put their own stamp on the learning endeavor. In turn, this leads to development of variations, experiments to test out emerging hypotheses and generalizations in new situations. Organizations that have made good use of Multiple Advocates, such as Motorola, consider it to be one of the first things to develop when beginning a new learning initiative.

Important questions to consider when working in this area include the following:

- How do we get senior management to support multiple ways of doing things?

- What is the permissible range of possibilities for policies and procedures? Can we find a middle ground between one method for all and each person having a different method?

- Are there ways to show that important results can be achieved through different means?

- How can we show that diversity of people is a support for learning rather than a problem calling for homogenization?

- What is the best way to teach people how to build coalitions without being seen as revolutionaries?

Operational Variety

Possible actions to increase Operational Variety include the following:

- Support ways of doing things that are different from the norm; hold people to firm targets but allow them to get there as they desire.

- Create more than one competence model for manager selection and development. Make room for different appealing role models.

- Try out parallel or sequential methods to see what each has to offer (two simultaneous production methods, a different approach in different marketing areas, and the like).

- In diversity efforts emphasize what can be learned from differences.

- Create policies with flexible alternatives (flexible bene-fit packages, flextime, and the like).

- Create work groups composed of diverse people.

Multiple Advocates

Actions that support Multiple Advocates include the following:

- Encourage people at all levels to bring in new ideas from outside the unit and to suggest new ways of learning.

- Support the expression of ideas that seem "far out" or radical.

- Arrange to have anyone who attends a conference or external education event discuss what was learned, present a formal report, or both.

- Before going far with it, identify people who have interest or skill in an area you wish to promote and recruit them to assist in the effort.

- Teach people how to form coalitions for development of any initiative.

- Educate senior people in the unit about the usefulness of "gatekeepers," those who bring new knowledge into the organization.

Summary

In this chapter we present a way of making choices and generating action plans for building learning capability at each of the three phases in the organizational learning cycle. We raise numerous questions and make suggestions for how you might proceed to implement a program designed to enhance performance on fourteen of the elements in our framework. At this point you may feel somewhat overwhelmed by the amount of material and number of lists in the preceding pages. Or you may feel that we stop short of providing practical solutions. Our objective has been to provide a framework and some guidelines and to avoid sounding righteous by telling you that you must do one thing or another. We prefer to provide a stimulus for your own deliberations and solutions that fit your own setting.

The philosophy stated here is consistent with the values of a capability and developmental perspective. From a normative perspective, however, we will become more righteous and suggest that any organization can benefit from improvement in the ten Facilitating Factors that we describe. This means that we can all strive to be better against some acceptable standard. We certainly support this, especially in light of the large number of poor learning organizations that we have observed. The capability perspective tells us that what is ideal for one firm, or for any given unit within a company, is not necessarily appropriate for another. To build organizational capability, the challenge is to utilize an integrated strategy that combines generic best practices with established competence.

9

Assessing Learning Capability Over Time

Building learning capability is a long-term task. In fact, some theorists have suggested that the mark of a good learning organization is a heightened awareness of the importance of continual learning and of making periodic assessments of learning progress. This chapter looks at how assessment can contribute to the building process.

As we progress on any journey, starting with a single step, we observe many wondrous and novel surroundings. With each step, the world takes on a different look as we see new places and new faces. We also see ourselves reflected back from the eyes and faces of those we meet. Such visions portray images of where we have been and how far we have come along our path. In the process, without ever asking a question, we begin to wonder how far we have actually journeyed and how far we have yet to go. Such wonder may emanate from simple curiosity or from concern about the sufficiency of our supplies, our energy, or our will. The more precise and anxious among us will seek assurance that our efforts are taking us where we want to go.

Inevitably we look for signs or guideposts along our path to satisfy our curiosity or concern. In building organizational learning capability, what signs should we look for and how do we interpret what we see? These and other questions are the subject of this chapter. As we build capability, it is important to acknowledge our progress while affirming or reexamining the desirability of our path and its direction.

The Relativity of Progress

In organizations, when we stop to consider how far we have come in any journey there are two critical dimensions that shape our inquiry: who is making the journey and what progress has been made at any given time. The first dimension deals with the entity involved. Whose progress is being measured, recorded, or understood? Are we examining what a single work team has learned or how that work team has expanded its learning capability? Or is the boundary of our focus drawn more widely to encompass multiple teams, departments, or an entire firm? It is important to define as clearly as possible the space around what is being measured, around who or what is taking the journey. Unit or level of analysis is a critical issue here in specifying whether the progress being measured is represented in the behavior of individuals, teams, or entire organizations or firms.

The other critical dimension that shapes any inquiry into progress is time. There are two aspects to this: the present relative to the past, and the present relative to where we expect to be or want to be in the future. The present is a relative point in time. The relativity comes from having progressed into the present from the past. Thus to consider what learning capabilities a team or firm has now that it did not have before requires knowing the team's starting point, or baseline. Once we determine how far a team has come from that baseline, we must then make our second assessment and consider how that present point of progress compares to where the team wants to be.

A team may progress a great deal (relative to the past) but yet still be far behind (relative to where it wants to be). After we have determined a team's relative progress in developing learning capability, we can state an opinion or make some judgment about our satisfaction over the progress that has been made. To do so involves taking into consideration why the team progressed the way it did. What internal and external factors led the team to increase its learning capability? Given those factors, should we be pleased or disappointed at the outcome?

Distinguishing Indicators of Learning Capability from the Assessment Process

A customary approach to monitoring the impact of any intervention or assessing progress is to pick several landmarks or indicators and see if they have been reached or realized. For example, if we know the way to San Jose we simply identify several places along the route and then know how far we have come as we pass each of those checkpoints. Unfortunately, building learning capability within our teams and organizations is not so simple.

What We Measure or Monitor Versus How

As the Hawthorne effect reminds us, when we pay attention to people, we affect them in some way, if only unintentionally. Assessing progress in the building of learning capability is itself an intervention because attention given to a team can affect its performance. As a form of feedback, assessment involves some form of examination from external sources or team introspection. In either case, the attention given to the team in the assessment process may alter the team's awareness of itself, its surroundings, or its expectations or desires. Certain ways of conducting assessment are more obtrusive or disruptive than others. In designing mechanisms to monitor impact, it is therefore imperative to consider not merely what will be measured but how that measurement will be done.

The decision about how to monitor progress must be linked to the question of why the assessment is being performed in the first place and why the journey to building learning capability was undertaken. Oftentimes the information needs of the observer or evaluator will vary from, if not conflict with, those of the observed or the evaluated. There are three basic reasons for assessing progress:

1. *To generate data to test or validate a theory.* Outside observers or academic researchers may be interested in measuring a team or firm's progress from a "scientific" perspective. Such research may serve to validate some theory about what builds learning capability and would require the generation of unbiased, objective data. The data are used to test or revise the researcher's theory about learning or change. When assessment is done as part of an action research project, the theory being tested may pertain to a staff or local theory specific to the firm.

2. *To evaluate progress relative to a goal.* Even in the midst of a journey there is still time to fine-tune or redirect efforts to reach the target. This approach to assessing progress, also known as "formative evaluation," is an opportunity to figure out what has worked and what has not and to make midcourse corrections. The evaluation can be used to ensure that the team is moving toward its goal and has the necessary resources for doing so. Underlying this approach to assessment is often a command and control mentality. Assessment is conducted to identify deviations from desired performance and to determine what actions are needed to get the team or organization back on track.

3. *To create dialogue leading to change.* Because the process of assessment is as important as what the assessment focuses on, that process can itself either impede or hasten the journey. One reason for conducting an assessment is to stimulate thinking and action. The process of doing an assessment creates dialogue among stakeholder groups and thereby increases their awareness of and sensitivity to critical issues. How the information generated by the assessment is used is determined by the needs of those groups themselves.

Approaches to Assessment

Since the advent of the learning organization concept, scholars and practitioners have designed a variety of measurement tools to assess learning organization characteristics and progress in becoming a learning organization. The popularity of mechanisms to measure learning has been so great that in 1996 the American Society of Training and Development published a guidebook describing eighteen different instruments. In general, each of these instruments is based on considering the learning organization within one of the three perspectives discussed in Chapter One. Each of the perspectives for developing learning in organizations considers the assessment process in slightly different terms.

Assessing Progress Within the Normative View

The focal point for intervention within the normative view is those factors or conditions that must be present in order for learning to take place. The assumption is that once present, these conditions ensure or represent learning. Thus to assess progress in building learning capability involves first identifying those critical conditions or traits and then testing for their relative presence or absence. For example, Peter Senge claims that learning organizations practice five disciplines. Given that framework, progress in building learning capability involves simply testing for the presence and quality of those disciplines within the team or organization. The assessment may be done by resources that are internal or external relative to the group whose progress is being measured.

Assessing Progress Within the Developmental View

The notion of progress is intrinsic to a developmentalist view of building learning capability. Organizations and teams progress through stages and, in so doing, alter their learning styles and competences. Assessment focuses on those factors or conditions that together characterize a developmental stage. The pattern of those characteristics represents the team or organization's stage; assessing progress focuses on determining the current stage and contrasting it with some previous position.

Assessing Progress Within the Capability View

The capability view emphasizes understanding the present and making explicit what might be hidden or overlooked. Of the three perspectives, it has the greatest focus on current competences. Progress is considered only within the framework of a set of competences or processes that characterize learning. A more distinctive feature of a capabilities perspective in measuring progress pertains to how the assessment is made. The emphasis here is on using the capabilities of the group, team, or organization itself to do the assessment and not rely on the viewpoint of any so-called objective outside experts.

The Integrated Approach to Assessing Organizational Learning Capability

Assessing organizational learning capability from an integrated approach implies taking aspects of each of the three frameworks and using them to build a more comprehensive approach. Such assessments incorporate the following:

1. A set of normative elements or factors that serve as guideposts along the path

2. A developmental framework for assessing learning capability over time

3. A process that enables team members to generate their own assessment of current and desired capabilities

To address the need to measure progress within an integrated approach, we developed a way to combine these three perspectives. Using the seventeen elements in our integrated framework, we designed an interactive process to profile the current and desired learning capabilities of an organizational unit, such as a department, work group, task force, or company subsidiary. To aid in the process and to serve as an intervention and vehicle for dialogue, we created a group exercise in which members of an organization, working with assistance from a trained facilitator, complete an assessment of the seventeen elements. This stimulates group discussion and provides an opportunity for group members to share knowledge and perceptions about their own learning practices. The result is an increased awareness of learning issues that provides a basis for constructive action. By giving recognition to existing although perhaps transparent capabilities, the group is able to use that awareness as a take-off point for desired competences. By engaging in this process at periodic intervals, the unit is provided with a developmental history and an evaluation of its progress.

To aid in the assessment process, we developed an assessment tool, the Organizational Learning Inventory (OLI). Guided by an experienced facilitator, members of a group follow the OLI to create their organizational learning profile, as exhibited in Chapter Six. The profile is created through dialogue among group members who share their knowledge and perceptions about the group's learning. The learning profile gives the group a starting point from which to build its learning capability, and the generation of the profile is itself an intervention and a process of group learning. The task of creating the profile establishes a process whereby group members of the team share information about what and how the group learns.

Issues in Assessing Progress in Building Learning Capability

As mentioned earlier in this chapter, a critical issue in assessing progress is placing boundaries around the work unit whose progress is being assessed. For all the talk of building learning capability within a team, what is a team? Many definitions are available in the literature, but we define a team as a bounded set of individuals acting interdependently to achieve a shared outcome.

Much of the work of large, complex organizations is performed by teams. The challenge facing most organizations is not whether to use teams to get the work done but how to use them most effectively. It is important to know what type of teams to create, how to organize and support teamwork, how to make the transition to greater teamwork, and how to manage an enterprise organized around teams.

Organizations generally are structured around individuals, functions, departments, or networks as the basic work group. A team is usually a subset of a work unit that is responsible for localized tasks. As organizations have become more complex, they also use cross-functional teams, task forces, and networks that may include people from several firms.

Whatever the unit, ideally all members work through the assessment process together. However, as the size of a group increases, the dialogue generated to create the learning profile becomes increasingly more difficult to process. Larger work groups also have more complex dynamics; common tendencies such as self-censorship can affect what learning profile the group will ultimately create. When a group has more than eight members, it is often best to split it into subgroups that each generate a learning profile. The total group can then come back together to discuss differences, if any, in the profiles created by the subgroups and to collectively generate a desired profile and set of action plans.

Another way the process has been used is to facilitate learning across an entire firm. As work groups and organizations can be successful with different learning styles, it is not unusual to find different learning styles within an entire firm; such differences can create problems for learning across a firm. In this context, multiple groups generate a set of learning profiles that represent the firm's different operational areas. Then, in a conference or workshop format, staff from these different areas can review the implications of the firm's learning portfolio as represented by the set of profiles.

The different ways of using the integrated assessment approach obviously lead to different outcomes. When the focus is exclusively on the learning processes within a single team or work group, then the dialogue generated becomes a team-building tool. However, when used across a firm with multiple groups, organizations, or subsidiaries, the process becomes a vehicle for organization development and for building learning capability between operational areas. The latter is especially important for firms that replicate similar tasks at multiple sites, such as franchises, chain stores, or manufacturing facilities. In this context, lessons from operational experience at one site should be transferred to another in order to share best practices or avoid the costly duplication of errors.

In either case, the process is used in a manner consistent with organizational development principles. One key is to recognize existent learning processes; another is to elicit and use the collective knowledge within a group. When group members or company employees participate in a shared process to define learning needs, the resultant solution will be more meaningful and more effective, and change implementation will produce more lasting results.

New or Existing Units

An important condition affecting the assessment process is the scope of a unit's experience together. Building learning capability is an altogether different process when a team, task force, department, network, or company is newly formed rather than well established. Two critical implications of these types of groups are the ease of generating the current profile of learning capability and that of developing a realistic action plan to move the work unit to a desired profile. Learning Orientations describe the culturally established ways by which a group, work unit, or organization acquires, disseminates, and uses knowledge. Intact teams with established ways of working together will find it much easier to generate their profile of LOrs than will a new team. Also, members of a new team or work unit may not be familiar with one another and thus may be uncomfortable openly discussing any barriers to learning that exist. However, new units may want to consider the characteristics of the culture they wish to create.

It is important to consider the history of a team's work together, especially the clarity of purpose, amount of contact, level of interdependencies, organizational alignment, and stability of membership. An established team may very well have some of the same characteristics of a new team, especially if its purpose or membership has shifted frequently. A new team will be more challenged than an existing team in generating its profile of current capabilities but may find it easier to generate a profile of desired capabilities. Established groups may be self-satisfied and unable to identify learning shortcomings or may have settled into such a routine of working together as to be uninterested in change. Established work units, then, may suffer from inertia or myopia that undermine interest in change. They may also find action planning more difficult than do new teams. Vested interests and personal concerns may conflict with changes that the group needs to make to improve learning capability; new teams are less apt to carry such "baggage."

Learning Profiles as Assessment Data

A learning profile contains seventeen data points, one for each Learning Orientation and Facilitating Factor. These data can be displayed on a flip chart, white board, or overhead transparency. Although it is important to examine each data point discretely, the profile represents the learning capability of a complete system. Hence it is as important to examine the pattern or configuration of data points as to look at each data point individually.

Our research indicates that there are some synergies between the Facilitating Factors. Work groups that are good at one FF are apt to be good at others. The profile data can also be examined in terms of relationships between LOrs and FFs. Theoretically these sets of elements are distinct, but specific groups may associate some of the elements together. For example, a work group that is positioned as mostly external on the first LOr (Knowledge Source) could rank itself high on the first FF (Scanning Imperative).

Current Profile and Best Profile

In developing our integrated approach, we have worked with teams to generate and interpret their profile data. Our experience indicates that teams and facilitators will confront a series of issues and decision points. For example, it is extremely common—indeed it should be expected—that once a team has generated its profile it will look to a facilitator for an opinion about the relative merits of that profile. In effect, team members conceive of some "best" profile for their team or organization and wonder how their current profile approximates it. This concern raises several critical issues in building learning capability.

First, is there an ideal profile? Is there a best profile for a particular group? As our integrated approach is based on a pluralistic view of learning styles, there is no universally ideal profile. That is not to say that some profiles are not better than others for a particular group, but how can we determine which ones? Better profiles can be derived from theoretical determination based on the nature of a group's work and a thorough understanding of the Learning Orientations. For example, work groups that function in changing environments should be positioned with a Knowledge Source that is more or mostly external.

When searching for the ideal profile for a particular group, a facilitator must be careful, as the group may force him or her out of the facilitator role and into that of the expert. Groups will look to the facilitator to provide an expert opinion of their ideal profile and an evaluation of how close their current profile is to that ideal. The facilitator may indeed offer some ideas about ideal profiles, but should step back and let the group determine its own ideal.

The desired outcome from use of an integrated strategy is group action. Such action is bound to be compromised if the facilitator takes on the role of expert and tells the group what its profile should be. The facilitator should encourage each group to generate a profile that it will own and that will lead it to action. In effect, the best profile is not determined by a theoretical optimum. What is sought is a profile that is generated by the work group, is realistic and feasible, and will lead to action. A desired profile that can be implemented is better than one that is theoretically better but impractical.

As there are so many ways to achieve organizational learning capability or to become a learning organization, methods to assess progress along the path need to echo this relativity. Such efforts should consider not simply what indicators of progress go into a team's learning profile but how that assessment or profile is generated and used. However, once a team or an entire firm takes action on specific factors essential to learning, then any assessment should focus on those same factors. The complexity of assessment derives from the relativity of the learning process, which varies by industry and environment. The next chapter shows how our integrated approach can be adapted to different contexts.

Part III

Adapting and Assessing
the Learning Strategy

10

Using an Integrated Strategy
in Different Contexts

O ur strategy can be used for developing tools and interventions
that are customized to specific industry or professional contexts. This chapter describes how we adapted our framework to the
health care industry and how our strategy can be used in different
situations. The key to adapting our strategy is to identify the stylistic, descriptive ways by which learning takes place within the specific context and then to identify those best practices that promote
or facilitate learning. Underlying this strategy is the notion that
teams and organizations have innate capabilities that can be developed over time and that through the efforts of team and organizational members themselves such capabilities can be developed
further.

Different Contexts Mean Different Cultures

Learning processes are fundamental ways by which culture is created and shared. To use the term "learning culture" might ignore
the fact that culture and learning cannot be separate from one
another. We enter this world as newborns and learn over time how
to function in a given society. We even learn how to learn. Acculturation is a natural process whereby we acquire and share culture
with others. This capability allows us to participate in colleagueship
with others in a social context.

Culture has been used historically to demark different societies from one another. Since the early 1980s culture has also been used as a way to differentiate organizations and companies from one another. The acculturation process that we experience in becoming a member of a society is an essential learning process that subsequently allows us to join or participate in different organizations. New employees of a company must learn its culture in order to fit in. This is not to say that the culture of a corporation or organization is somehow separate from the social context in which it is embedded. For example, EMC Corporation, a high-tech designer and manufacturer of computer storage devices, recently tried to recruit staff from among football fans because many of its employees support EMC's local pro football team.

In defining culture as a set of shared assumptions, values, and artifacts, Edgar Schein (1992) pointed out that an organization's culture cannot be analyzed prior to our confrontation with it. Otherwise we impose our externally generated categories of culture to understand the culture of another group or society. To understand how learning takes place in one cultural context or organization, we need to develop mechanisms to profile learning with dimensions that are consistent with that context. How a group of engineers learn together, for example, would differ markedly from how a group of product marketing managers learn together. Such a statement, consistent with a pluralistic notion that learning can occur successfully in a variety of ways, acknowledges that there are many reasons why and how learning occurs and diversity in what can be learned.

Based on research in a diverse set of companies, we generated our initial set of seven Learning Orientations to represent the culturally defined processes whereby learning takes place in the context of those companies and organizations. That framework of seven LOrs is a generic set of dimensions that we have found to be generally applicable to many company and team contexts. However, variations in culture across teams and across industries create a less than perfect fit for our framework in some contexts. To use an integrated strategy in specific contexts requires some adaptation of the specific elements of our framework to make it more easily understood by the participants and culture holders of those diverse contexts.

Part of the adaptation process involves the recognition of idiosyncrasies of language and of concepts of culture that have meaning in one industry or team context but not in another. Such differences are essential to acknowledge in order to develop a framework for describing the learning processes that exist in a given team or organizational context. Thus there is a need not only to adapt the language of learning but also the very specific ways in which learning processes take place.

Different contexts of learning also engender different leverage points for changing learning. Thus in considering the normative element of our framework, the Facilitating Factors, we need to acknowledge that in different contexts learning is promoted for different reasons. Thus adapting to or using our framework in a given context requires a review of the specific FFs or best practices that engender learning. To generate a learning profile for a particular context may require a review of the elements in our integrated framework as well as the development of specific examples that reflect the nature of learning in those different contexts. By creating or acknowledging such differences, a learning inventory can be adapted or utilized in a fashion that is most helpful and appropriate to a given team or company context.

Learning Mechanisms in Different Industries and Professions

Different industries and professions have distinctive mechanisms to promote learning capability. For example, in the field of civil aviation the National Transportation Safety Board (NTSB) acts in concert with aircraft designers, manufacturers, and operators to develop procedures and protocols that will allow learning to take place over time and to improve the overall safety of the airline industry. In this way, the NTSB operates as a community of practice to both formally and informally share knowledge within the industry about best practices based on learning experiences.

In the nuclear power field, the Institute for Nuclear Power Operations (INPO), created after the nuclear accident that occurred at the Three Mile Island plant in 1976, serves in a similar fashion. Among its many functions, INPO takes the operating experience from a diverse set of nuclear power operators and disseminates knowledge gained from that experience in order to improve the operation of nuclear power plants not only in the United States but in the rest of the world as well.

In some industries the mechanisms to promote learning derive from internal factors, such as the desire for industry members to increase their effectiveness relative to competing industries. In other industries the mechanisms are stimulated by action in the public sector. Consumer affairs groups and consumer safety councils are mechanisms to promote learning from public experience in using various consumer products. In the field of education, accreditation boards, whose main function is certifying the quality of education, also act as a mechanism for institutions to reflect on their experiences and determine how they should better learn about what has been done successfully in the past.

In some industries the mechanisms for learning are not situated at a company-coordinated level but more at a professional level. For example, in the fields of law and medicine professional associations such as the American Bar Association and the American Medical Association provide forums for their members to share experiences about best practices and to recognize and reward the actions of professionals that reflect exemplary learning lessons, activities, or breakthroughs that come from such learning.

Using an Integrated Strategy in Health Care

The health care industry is among those currently undergoing significant pressure to change. Change is occurring not solely because of tremendous cost pressures and the number of mergers and shifts in alliances between providers, organizations, and patients or customers but because the very nature and definition of the health care business is being challenged.

In the past the industry was dominated by a large number of players who considered themselves to be in the nonprofit service sector; now economic pressures are increasing on the for-profit side. Concurrently, questions have been raised about the role of health care. The issue is whether health care should play more of a curative role, reacting to sickness, or a proactive role, ensuring that illness does not occur in the first place.

The result of all this is a tremendous need for teams and organizations in health care to increase and develop their learning capabilities. In order to provide the industry with a tool that would facilitate the development of learning capability, the Healthcare Forum became familiar with our integrated strategy and asked us to adapt and apply it to the specific circumstances and challenges facing health care today. The presumption up front was that health care is an extremely different—indeed unique—industry for which the elements in our framework would have little relevance. In fact, though health care has a set of distinctive features, it does represent a generic context in which work takes place and learning occurs. Health care providers and organizations have idiosyncrasies in their language and specific concepts, but the industry is situated in a larger economic system that shares many characteristics.

To adapt our integrated strategy to the health care context, we conducted a series of in-depth field studies in six health care settings. In the process we came to recognize that there are indeed some distinctive features of learning in health care that differ from what we had earlier identified in the case studies that led to our initial framework. The differences are in both how learning takes place and, more critically, why learning takes place—the best practices that promote learning.

The Learning Orientations of Health Care Systems

One of our seven Learning Orientations stood out like a sore thumb, so to speak, for professionals in health care: Value-Chain Focus. This has to do with the notion that companies can spend time to design and make products and services and that there is a process whereby those products and services ultimately are shaped and delivered to customers and clients. The line from design-and-make at one end to market-and-deliver at the other is the value chain, and different points along it represent different learning investments that a company can make. For health care professionals, however, the value-chain concept makes little, if any, sense.

As we came to understand how learning takes place in health care, we recognized that the field has cultural characteristics that do not match the seven LOrs in our generic framework. In effect, health care culture has several distinctive properties that affect organizational learning capability. However, most of the LOrs did make sense and did represent what we saw in our case studies of health care situations. Yet some adaptations were required to make the LOrs fit or make sense to health care professionals. For example, whereas the first version of our framework labeled the second LOr "Product-Process Focus," in health care the product is most often a service. Thus we retained the LOr but changed the label to "Content-Process Focus," reflecting the likelihood that health care will provide a service rather than a tangible product.

More critical than the refinement or relabeling of some of our LOrs was the addition of two new ones that reflect the unique conditions health care staff must operate in. The first of these is Learning Timeframe, defined as the emphasis on learning that responds to immediate needs as compared to learning that may have long-term use. The polar extremes on the continuum of this Learning Orientation are "immediate" and "long-term."

Some of the learning that takes place in health care contexts involves practices or techniques that are used immediately in providing services to either diagnose or respond to illness. Health care is a unique context in which the effect of not learning (possible death) is so critical and significant that professionals continually explore new technologies, procedures, and protocols of intervention in order to cure their patients. Thus service providers learn new tools and techniques because they are needed immediately to address or possibly rectify a disease or illness that lacks a solution or is in need of a better one. By learning and using new techniques or procedures, health care providers may increase patient survival rates. Still, health care organizations must develop core competences over a longer term to distinguish themselves from their competitors. Thus learning must also focus on the development of long-term advantages and strategic needs.

The second added Learning Orientation is Learning Mode, defined as "generate and share knowledge and skills through action or practice as compared to generate and share knowledge and skills through reflective activities or thinking." This LOr represents a distinctive way in which learning takes place in health care. The two polar extremes on this dimension are "experiential" and "cognitive." This LOr represents the necessity for service providers to learn new techniques before they are thoroughly understood or known.

In health care there is a training tradition referred to as "see one, do one, teach one." However, rapid changes in technology mean that often a practitioner has little or no opportunity to actually see how a procedure or protocol is done before having to use it. This happens because experiments or simulations with human cadavers or other primates can only go so far in helping a practitioner understand how the procedure will work with a real, live patient. For example, Richard DeBakey, the first American physician to transplant a human heart, was able to test the procedure earlier on baboons and apes. But when it came to actually doing the procedure for the first time with a live human being he still had much to learn as he went through the experience.

However, much as there is a high rate of change in medical care, there also is a need for reflection and a thorough study of the advantages and disadvantages of different protocols. This leads to the need for a cognitive learning approach such that knowledge and solutions to problems can be generated before they are actually used in a clinical setting. The detailed procedures that must be followed to get drugs approved by the FDA are an effort to learn in a highly cognitive way so as to reduce the learning that will take place in real-life situations.

Each of these two approaches (experiential and cognitive) represents accepted ways of learning within health care. On the one hand, the need to take some action to cure or relieve the suffering of a sick patient will necessitate experiential learning given the risks involved. On the other hand, the experience of dealing with many patients over time creates a set of experiences that can be analyzed and used to develop learning that is then communicated in a formal way outside of the demands and emergencies of a given situation.

Facilitating Factors in Health Care

Examining the normative side of our integrated strategy as it applies to health care met with similar results. There was high overlap between the Facilitating Factors identified prior to our work in health care and those that promote learning in health care. Some definitions and labels had to be changed to account for the idiosyncrasies of the language and lexicon of health care professionals, but a few new factors had to be added as well. The most important and significant change in labeling involved the fifth FF, Climate of Openness. The way this factor was described within health care pertains to the amount of trust and open communication between colleagues and the respect that team members have for mutual growth and development. Health care staff changed the label of this factor to Trusting Relationships, and they considered it the single most important factor that leads to learning. When you trust your colleagues, you can be open about explaining not only your successes but also your failures. Within that context of support and mutual respect, a practitioner can take risks to learn, realizing that those around you will appreciate you for the effort you made even should your action fall short of its goal. Furthermore, as pointed out in research by Edmondson (1996), errors are more apt to be reported, detected, and corrected when there is trust among health care practitioners.

In trying to understand why learning takes place in our research settings, we identified three additional Facilitating Factors that explain it. The first is Learning Confidence, which we defined as "experience in learning from successes, mistakes, and specific events; experience in trying new things; belief that all groups can learn." In effect, Learning Confidence is a sort of lag variable that represents historical precedent: if you have learned in the past you are apt to have confidence that you can learn in the present. This amounts to skill in addressing an area of unknown competence with conviction and confidence that the skill it involves can be acquired and learned. This factor allows health care service providers to engage in new protocols and techniques and to assign them to teams and groups that may not have utilized them previously. Given the major changes that have occurred in health care over the last fifty years, it is hard to ignore the validity of this factor. Consider, for example, the frequency of organ transplants and heart bypass surgeries; they were much less common ten or twenty years ago but now occur so often that we rarely hear about them.

A second Facilitating Factor that could not be overlooked in the health care context was Shared Vision. The notion of Shared Vision is critical to the health care industry because of its historical focus on mission and service to community and humankind. Whereas certain industries (increasingly the health care industry too) are being asked to measure their performance on the basis of specific quantitative measures of profitability, health care has historically considered itself to be focusing on a different measure of success. Given the changes that are occurring within the health care industry now, learning on a team level occurs because values and vision are shared within the team.

Considering how popular the television show M*A*S*H was in its day, it may not come as a surprise that a third Facilitating Factor, Learning Enjoyment, was added to our list. The pace of change in health care and the critical demands caused by the need to do things exactly right (given the grave consequences for not doing so) create an environment where coping mechanisms are essential. Learning Enjoyment is defined as "celebrating learning achievements and creating an atmosphere where humor and fun are part of the process of acquiring new knowledge." Failures and mistakes are life-and-death matters in health care, and unless some humor and lightness can be brought to the sharing of such occurrences, there is apt to be little sharing of the lessons learned from such events. Humor is a critical coping mechanism that, when legitimized, not only adds to the playfulness and experimental mode of inquisitiveness but also allows for the open sharing of information that prevents errors and problems from being glossed over.

Figure 10.1 (pp. 190–191) contains the organizational learning profile for health care. It includes the twenty-one elements specifically designed for use in the health care industry. This set of elements can provide a clear basis for health care teams and organizations to profile existing learning capabilities and to provide focus on how those capabilities can be developed further.

Using the Integrated Strategy in Diverse Settings with Teams and Organizations

The purpose of the integrated strategy is to increase awareness and understanding of the practices that contribute to learning and improved performance within organizations—and to identify ways to improve those capabilities. Most of the research and development that created this approach focused on intact organizational teams. However, it can also be used in other types of team situations. Using the integrated strategy with different teams leads to different experiences, opportunities, and challenges. It is important to recognize the different dynamics that occur in working with different types of teams and the different outcomes that can be expected.

Single Teams Versus Multiple Teams

When building learning capability with teams from different parts of an organization, it is important to understand their interdependencies. The actual configuration of teams and their interests will determine their ability to create and follow through on a collective plan of action. It is a relatively straightforward process to review the pattern of a single team's learning profile and discuss how it might wish to alter that profile and improve learning capability. However, with multiple groups from the same organization or firm the situation becomes significantly more complex.

To deal with such complexity, one option is to process the learning profiles of the multiple teams independently of one another. A facilitator could approach the teams separately, as if they did not operate within the same organization. Indeed, for reasons of politics or expediency or both this may sometimes be the only option available. However, this will usually produce suboptimal results, because it is almost certain that there are real systemic connections between teams or work groups in a single firm. A more productive and thus preferred approach is to consider the learning profiles of all the work units or teams collectively. Differences and similarities between profiles should be examined to understand problems or conflicts that teams have in working or learning from one another. For example, profiles should be looked at in terms of how specific elements (LOrs or FFs) may prevent or expedite the sharing of knowledge across teams.

When examining the learning profiles of multiple teams together, a facilitator should make observations (not necessarily judgments) about the similarities and differences between profiles. The facilitator should then solicit opinions and perspectives as to whether the observed differences or similarities are positive or negative. For example, differences may be negative if they block the sharing of knowledge but positive if they produce different types or processes of learning.

Figure 10.1. Learning Profile for Health Care

LEARNING
ORIENTATIONS

	MOSTLY	MORE	EVEN	MORE	MOSTLY	
1. Knowledge Source	INTERNAL						EXTERNAL
2. Content-Process Focus	CONTENT						PROCESS
3. Knowledge Reserve	PERSONAL						PUBLIC
4. Dissemination Mode	FORMAL						INFORMAL
5. Knowledge Focus	INCREMENTAL						TRANSFORMATIVE
6. Learning Timeframe	IMMEDIATE						LONG-TERM
7. Learning Focus	INDIVIDUAL						GROUP
8. Learning Mode	EXPERIENTIAL						COGNITIVE

FACILITATING FACTORS	Little evidence to support this factor		Some evidence to support this factor			Extensive evidence to support this factor	
	1	2	3	4	5	6	7
1. Performance Tension							
2. Trusting Relationships							
3. Leadership							
4. Systems Perspective							
5. Multiple Advocates							
6. Learning Confidence							
7. Organizational Curiosity							
8. Appreciation for Measurement							
9. Learning Resources							
10. Appreciation of Diversity							
11. Scanning Imperative							
12. Shared Vision							
13. Learning Enjoyment							

Staff Versus Line Teams

In our experience, line teams find the integrated strategy practical and use it as a team-building activity. However, staff teams are often concerned with the larger context of the strategy—its theoretical basis and validity, and how the rest of the organization or firm might "score" based on it. Alignment within the organization is a natural response from staff teams, given their functions. For a staff team the choice of an action planning approach may be more closely related to strategic issues, whereas a line team may be more interested in concrete operational problems. Line teams may be more inclined to value the team-building aspect of our integrated strategy because of their need for cohesion. Staff teams may be more interested in the connection of learning among teams within the organization and how any plan for building learning capability will work, be evaluated, and be linked with other organizational initiatives.

Teams and Organizations Involved in Mergers and Acquisitions

Teams involved in mergers and acquisitions often have characteristics similar to those of new teams, but with the added complexity of teams from multiple organizations (often with very different cultures). The integrated strategy provides an ideal method for teams from different organizations to examine their own learning styles and practices and an objective means for comparing organizational cultures. Like new teams, they then have the opportunity to define explicitly what characteristics may be required to make the merger or acquisition successful.

Factors that make it difficult for teams to come together include lack of a history of working together, lack of established processes for learning and performing, and the heightened sensitivity and emotional environment often associated with mergers. Creating learning profiles might be ideal for a small group of representatives from each organization; it may help them understand the learning capabilities of each and then create a desired profile for the merged entity. Insights generated from this process could form the foundation for a variety of action plans to support the merger.

Our work in difficult industries and firms and with different types of teams in diverse settings has demonstrated that the integrated strategy has wide applicability. The combination of descriptive and prescriptive elements gives teams and organizations a variety of entry points to build learning capability. The general framework also provides opportunity for further adaptation by customizing elements to particular contexts. This chapter explains the adaptive results when we used our strategy with health care professionals and how facilitators might use our ideas with different types of groups. We turn now to our final chapter and the question of learning outcomes.

11

Conclusion: What Is the Good of All This Learning?

Assessing the Impact of Learning on Performance

The key objective in building organizational learning capability is to maintain or improve team or organizational performance. Such improvement comes when a team or organization learns from its own experience or the experience of others. But how do we know that performance has improved? During a period when our time and other resources are limited, more and more people ask, What is the outcome? Why make the investment in organizational learning? Indeed, what is the benefit of learning and how do we know that it has occurred? Part of building organizational learning capability is the enhancement or creation of feedback loops to inform individuals, teams, and firms about the outcome of their actions. Such learning takes place through listening posts that provide a window to the outside world and the acquisition and sharing of knowledge that contributes to learning.

Several critical issues arise in considering learning outcomes. First is the distinction made at the very outset of this book regarding learning that leads to behavioral as opposed to cognitive change. If our desired outcome from learning is some behavioral change, such as the acquisition of certain skills, then empirical examination would reveal whether those behaviors occurred as a result of a learning intervention. However, learning may involve the acquisition of behaviors that would only be used in some emergency or specific set of circumstances. At the beginning of this book, we used the example of airplane passengers learning how to put on a life vest. Another example would be employees of a manufacturing facility learning how to vacate a building in case of fire. In these situations, we would not know whether these behaviors had been learned until such time as they actually had to be utilized.

This raises a second critical distinction in the assessment of learning outcomes: Are we looking at outcomes in the short or long term? Closely connected to the issue of term is the matter of attribution. If something good happens, should we attribute it to learning, to chance, or to some factor that is beyond anyone's control? "Learning lags" occur when we discover that an outcome we thought was satisfactory in fact was not. The lag occurs when significant time passes between when the action took place and when we learn whether the action was appropriate or not.

Consider two examples. I am a mortgage officer at a major metropolitan bank, and assessment of my performance is based on the number and dollar value of the loans that I sell to people and companies investing in real estate. To sell the loans I must satisfy a variety of bank requirements with regard to the qualifications of the buyer and the condition of the real estate being purchased. However, beyond those requirements I have a certain amount of discretion in approving loans. To maximize the volume of loans I sell, I may in fact authorize loans to individuals who subsequently forfeit or default on those loans. However, such defaults may not occur until four or five or many years after I authorized the loans, was promoted for the volume of loans I sold, and moved on to a higher position within the bank.

Or say that a maintenance worker at a nuclear power plant improperly assembles a pump or valve on a safety system. Once the plant is in operation the reactor building is sealed, and no one is in a position to realize or learn that the safety system is improperly set up. Only when the safety system needs to be deployed is it found that the behavior of the maintenance worker was improper—that behavior we thought had been learned in fact had not been.

Sometimes we consider learning to have taken place simply because no problems or accidents have occurred. The absence of an undesirable outcome is used as an indicator of learning. If problems do occur, we presume that something that should have been learned, such as how to maintain an aircraft engine, was not. A related indicator is the lack of recurrence of previous problems or errors. If an organization has learned from its experience, then problems should not recur.

Outcomes from the activities and efforts of organizations and work teams derive from so many different factors, particularly if we take a systems view, that it is sometimes hard to make a direct connection between learning efforts and their outcomes. Perhaps the only true way to measure the outcome of learning is to compare the outcomes that derive from learning efforts with those situations in which no learning effort is made. In effect, what is the cost of not learning? It may be important to distinguish outcomes that occur as a result of what is to be learned from outcomes that derive from learning as a process that has value by itself.

The difficulty of being 100 percent sure about learning outcomes and attributing outcomes to specific learning efforts requires that organizations and teams customize their own learning outcomes and measures. In effect, teams must take a contingent approach to determine what being a learning organization means to them and what outcomes they want to derive from such efforts.

Figure 11.1 shows our two-part framework in the context of both business and social outcomes. Business outcomes may consist of traditional corporate concerns such as profitability, return on equity, or market share. More immediate learning outcomes may simply be improved work processes that reduce production errors or product defects.

Yet there is a larger issue about learning outcomes that pertains to their social effects. As our businesses build learning capability,

Figure 11.1.   Learning Capabilities and Outcomes

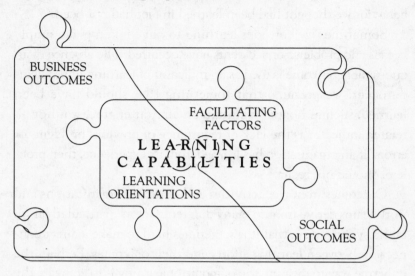

what are the direct and indirect consequences? Many firms today talk about becoming learning organizations. Do firms want to become learning organizations to improve profitability, the quality of work life for their employees, or the quality of life for society at large? We do not think business and social outcomes of learning can be looked at separately. For example, the learning that has taken place within the computer industry about how to miniaturize information storage has had a social impact ranging from the creation of virtual money and phone cards to the development of cellular phones, pagers, and other handheld electronic devices. 3M's Post-It notes are another example of a product innovation that came from learning capability and that had positive business and social outcomes.

The learning capabilities our businesses build and the learning investments they make can have a significant impact on society. Learning investments are made not only by the business sector but by governments and by partnerships between business and government. Perhaps if the National Railroad Administration could build learning capability, Amtrak could reduce its deficit (business outcome) and our trains would be more reliable (social outcome). During World War II the United States government invested in the Manhattan Project to support the efforts of scientists to learn how to make a functional atomic bomb. The outcome has had tremendous social, economic, and political impact. What our organizations learn is thus important not simply to those doing the learning but to those on whom it will have an impact. If our public and private organizations focused their learning investments on issues of common concern, such as public safety, and did so in a coordinated way, perhaps we could learn new solutions to such problems. Indeed, the complexity of today's social problems calls out for coordinated learning. A social history of the world shows that when we face a common enemy (as the Allied forces did in World War II) or share a common vision (such as placing a man on the moon) we can learn together. Both these examples show the presence of a clear, identifiable learning outcome.

One of the difficulties in identifying and measuring learning outcomes is that learning itself becomes transparent over time, and we fail to recognize what we have learned or accomplished, such as harnessing the power of the atom or walking on the moon. A related problem is that we are rarely aware of what we do not know and what we need to learn. Thus the recent efforts by companies in a variety of contexts to develop learning networks or networks of companies that learn in collaboration with one another are highly significant. Rather than learning in isolation, with the possibility of developing a myopic or a not-invented-here view of the world, companies are forming alliances in order to learn with other companies. For example, the Marketing Science Institute is a collaborative effort of more than sixty major corporations that conducts research on a variety of issues that pertain to marketing. The lessons derived from their research are generally function-specific, but there are other collaborative efforts in which learning takes place throughout an industry. The Institute for Nuclear Power Operations in Atlanta, Georgia, which creates lessons for companies that design, build, and maintain nuclear power plants, is a particular case in point.

Other collaborative efforts are cross-industry, such as the International Corporate Learning Association (InterClass), the International Consortium for Executive Development Research (ICEDR), and the Institute for Research on Learning (IRL). InterClass is a consortium of fifteen firms that meet regularly to discuss and learn about business problems and solutions. ICEDR, which supported our initial research, is another example of this type of learning alliance arrangement; it has thirty-five corporate members and twenty-five institutional or university members. IRL promotes collaborative learning alliances among a wide range of public, business, and educational organizations. Its focus on communities of practice is particularly suited to making visible and leveraging the inherent learning of social systems, an emphasis characteristic of a capability perspective. As this chapter is being written, a professional association, the Society for Organizational Learning (SOL), is being formed as a spinoff from the MIT Center for Organizational Learning. SOL will bring together corporations, researchers, and consultants to collaboratively develop new learning theories and techniques.

These collaborative efforts, or learning networks, actually comprise communities of practice in which individuals come together to share stories and experiences in a public context, with the notion that such efforts can generate new insight. Another strategy or tactic used to engender learning in a collective context is "open space" or "future search." Here, individuals from a given company or related companies or constituencies come together to learn about one another's values and shared vision, and how their collaborative efforts are required in our interdependent world in order to realize that vision.

Learning as an Intervention

For more than ten years, instituting Total Quality Management (TQM) has been a focus of intervention for many practitioners of organization development (OD). A major aspect of TQM is continuous improvement processes that represent ways in which organizations learn to be more efficient. Such increased efficiency may come from the learning created by a company's own operations (internal Knowledge Source) or through benchmarking activities (external Knowledge Source). However, in these changing times a firm's competitive advantage comes not only from getting better at what it already does but from learning about new products, new markets, or entirely new performance techniques. As firms and organizations create the conditions for learning, there is an emerging need for tools that measure, diagnose, or assess learning capability.

Two traditional values of OD practice have been to recognize the potential contribution and worth of each and every individual and to affirm the benefits gained from having individuals work together in groups. Many approaches to organizational learning are based on an opposing set of values that focuses on human shortcomings and group learning disabilities. Such approaches follow a normative path by claiming that organizations and groups cannot learn unless they follow some prescriptive model of intervention. Rather than presuming that there is something wrong in most organizations (consistent with a medical intervention model to treat or cure illness and disease), practitioners should base their approach on a wellness model: that learning processes and potential exist in most organizations as social systems. Instead of diagnosing and evaluating an organization to identify shortcomings based on a universal, normative model, an integrated strategy for organization development would recognize and legitimate alternative learning styles and processes.

By profiling an organization in terms of existent capabilities, practitioners—internal or external—may then choose ways to build upon those capabilities by incorporating member views on learning rather than emulate a prescribed, externally derived model or set of interventions. This strategy builds on the notion that acceptance of what has been accomplished is validating and energizing for those involved and is consistent with appreciative inquiry, an OD strategy advocated by some change agents (Srivastva, Cooperrider, and Associates, 1990). An OD strategy of organizational learning would also elicit team members' views about learning objectives and leverage points for change. Hence diagnosis becomes a way of learning about learning, and the generation of insight and the sharing of information about learning serve as interventions.

By recognizing existing although perhaps transparent capabilities, an integrated strategy empowers work teams and organizations to acknowledge the present but to use that awareness as a takeoff point for desired competences. Our set of seventeen elements provides a framework to uncover existing learning capabilities in organizations and to affirm rather than denigrate organizational experience. The learning profile gives a work team or set of organizations a starting point to build its learning capability, and the generation of the profile is itself an intervention and a process of team learning. The task of creating the profile establishes a process whereby group members of the team share information about what and how the team learns.

The Integrated Strategy as a Platform for Action

In the process of developing their profile of existing capabilities, groups inevitably discuss how their profile differs from what it may have been in the past and what they think it should be. This shared insight provides a starting point for groups to conduct action planning. Here the group goes back over the set of Learning Orientations and Facilitating Factors and instead of profiling current capabilities identifies desired capabilities. Action plans can be put together to identify strategies and tactics needed to reduce the gap between the desired and current profiles.

The two-part integrated framework provides groups with multiple change options. A group may first decide to focus on a particular stage of the learning cycle—knowledge acquisition, dissemination, or utilization. Then it may choose to change its style by shifting Learning Orientations, to improve its style through better performance on the Facilitating Factors, or to work on a combination of both types of elements. The key is to let a work team's own knowledge about the potentialities and leverage points for change guide the action planning process and to generate a work team or organization's desired learning profile. Instead of imposing a solution for developing learning capability, the integrated strategy prompts a work group to come up with its own problem definition (as reflected in the gap between the current and desired profiles) and the solution (action plans). In this way, the outcome will be a set of interventions that has staff ownership and builds upon the staff's own knowledge. What better way to intervene in any organizational system than by enhancing the capability of that system to understand itself and its learning processes?

In this book we present our integrated strategy. We hope to have done so in a manner that demystifies the vision of the learning organization by recognizing the transparent capabilities of all organizational systems to support learning processes. However, we must not forget that learning is not serendipitous but takes concerted action and effort. Here the Facilitating Factors provide a guide for how best to promote organizational learning. Our integrated strategy is a method for enhancing competitive advantage, but it is up to you, the reader, to determine how that advantage will be applied and used. Any weapon, tactic, or strategy can be used for promoting the common good or for furthering private gain. Which outcomes companies and work teams seek in using the integrated strategy will undoubtedly be linked to core values, culture, and sense of mission. In building learning capability that makes our companies become more competitive, we should act collaboratively and recognize that the best outcomes of learning are ones that enable us all.

References

Adler, P. S., and Cole, R. E. "Designed for Learning: A Tale of Two Auto Plants." *Sloan Management Review*, 1993, *34*, 85–94.

Allen, T. "Communication Networks in R&D Labs." *R&D Management*, 1971, *1*, 14–21.

Argyris, C. *Strategy, Change and Defensive Routines*. New York: Putnam, 1985.

Argyris, C., and Schön, D. A. *Organizational Learning*. Reading, Mass.: Addison-Wesley, 1978.

Bolton, M. K. "Imitation Versus Innovation." *Organizational Dynamics*, 1993, *21*, 30–45.

Boulding, K. E. *The Image*. Ann Arbor: University of Michigan Press, 1956.

Brown, J. S., and Duguid, P. "Organizational Learning and Communities of Practice." *Organization Science*, 1991, *2*, 40–57.

Cameron, K. S., and Whetten, D. A. "Models of the Organizational Life Cycle: Applications to Higher Education." *The Review of Higher Education*, 1983, *6*, 269–299.

Case, J. *Open-Book Management: The Coming Business Revolution*. New York: HarperCollins, 1995.

"Companies That Train Best." *Fortune*, Feb. 8, 1993, pp. 44–48.

Cyert, R. M., and March, J. G. *A Behavioral Theory of the Firm*. Englewood Cliffs, N.J.: Prentice Hall, 1963.

Darling, M., and Hennessy, G. "Charting a Corporate Learning Strategy." *The System Thinker*, 1995, *6*(10), 1–5.

Dechant, K., and Marsick, V. J. "In Search of the Learning Organization: Toward a Conceptual Model of Collective Learning." *Proceedings of the Eastern Academy of Management*. Hartford, Conn.: Eastern Academy of Management, 1991, 225–228.

Dertouzos, M., Lester, R., and Solow, R. *Made in America*. Cambridge, Mass.: MIT Press, 1989.

DiBella, A. J. "Developing Learning Organizations: A Matter of Perspective." Paper presented at the Academy of Management meeting, Vancouver, Canada, 1995.

DiBella, A. J., Nevis, E. C., and Gould, J. M. "Understanding Organizational Learning Capability." *Journal of Management Studies*, 1996, *33*, 361–379.

Edmondson, A. C. "Learning from Mistakes Is Easier Said Than Done: Group and Organizational Influences on the Detection and Correction of Human Error." *Journal of Applied Behavioral Science*, 1996, *32*(1), 5–28.

Gardner, H. *Multiple Intelligences: Theory in Practice*. New York: Basic Books, 1993.

Garratt, B. *Creating a Learning Organization: A Guide to Leadership, Learning, and Development*. New York: Simon & Schuster, 1990.

Garvin, D. A. "Building a Learning Organization." *Harvard Business Review*, July-Aug. 1993, pp. 78–91.

Goleman, D. *Emotional Intelligence*. New York: Bantam Books, 1995.

Greiner, L. E. "Evolutions and Revolution as Organizations Grow." *Harvard Business Review*, July-Aug. 1972, pp. 37–46.

Hamel, G., and Prahalad, C. K. *Competing for the Future*. Boston: Harvard Business School Press, 1994.

Hedberg, R. "How Organizations Learn and Unlearn." In N. C. Nystrom and W. H. Starbuck (eds.), *Handbook of Organizational Design*. Oxford: Oxford University Press, 1981.

Huber, G. P. "Organizational Learning: The Contributing Processes and the Literatures." *Organization Science*, 1991, *2*, 88–115.

Jelinek, M. *Institutionalizing Innovation: A Study of Organizational Learning Systems*. New York: Praeger, 1979.

Kaplan, R. S., and Norton, D. P. "The Balanced Scorecard: Measures That Drive Performance." *Harvard Business Review*, Jan.-Feb. 1992, pp. 71–79.

Katzenback, J. R., and Smith, D. K. *The Wisdom of Teams*. Boston: Harvard Business School Press, 1993.

Kimberly, J. "Issues in the Creation of Organizations: Initiation, Innovation, and Institutionalization." *Academy of Management Journal*, 1979, *22*, 437–457.

Kimberly, J., and Miles, R. *The Organizational Life-Cycle: Issues in the Creation, Transformation, and Decline of Organizations*. San Francisco: Jossey-Bass, 1980.

Kolb, D. A. "On Management of the Learning Process." In D. L. Rubin and F. McIntyre (eds.), *Organizational Psychology: A Book of Readings*. Englewood Cliffs, N.J.: Prentice Hall, 1979.

Kolind, L. "Thinking the Unthinkable." *Focus on Change Management*, Apr. 1994, pp. 4–9.

LaBarre, P. "The Dis-Organization of Oticon." *Industry Week*, July 18, 1994, pp. 23–28.

Lave, J., and Wenger, E. *Situated Learning: Legitimate Peripheral Participation*. New York: Cambridge University Press, 1991.

Leonard-Barton, D. "The Factory as a Learning Laboratory." *Sloan Management Review*, 1992, *34*, 23–38.

Lessem, R. *Total Quality Learning: Building a Learning Organization*. Oxford, England: Blackwell, 1991.

Lindbloom, C., and Cohen, D. *Usable Knowledge*. New Haven, Conn.: Yale University Press, 1979.

March, J. G., and Simon, H. A. *Organizations*. New York: Wiley, 1958.

March, J. G., Sproull, L. S., and Tamuz, M. "Learning from Samples of One or Fewer." *Organization Science*, 1991, *2*, 1–13.

Marsick, V., Dechant, K., and Kasl, E. "Group Learning Among Professionals: The Brewster Company Case Study." In *Professionals' Ways of Knowing and Implications for CPE: Proceedings of the Annual Conference*, Commission for Continuing Professional Education. Montreal: American Association of Adult and Continuing Education, 1991.

Mayo, A., and Rick, S. "Recognising a Learning Organization." *European Forum for Management Development*, 1993, *1*, 14–17.

McGill, M. E., and Slocum, J. W. "Unlearning the Organization." *Organizational Dynamics*, 1993, *22*, 67–78.

McGill, M. E., Slocum, J. W., and Lei, D. "Management Practices in Learning Organizations." *Organizational Dynamics*, 1992, *21*, 5–17.

McKee, D. "An Organizational Learning Approach to Product Innovation." *Journal of Product Innovation Management*, 1992, *9*, 232–245.

McNamara, R. *In Retrospect: The Tragedy and Lessons of Vietnam*. New York: Random House, 1995.

Meyers, P. W. "Non-Linear Learning in Large Technological Firms: Period Four Implies Chaos." *Research Policy*, 1990, *19*, 97–115.

"Motorola: Training for the Millenium." *Business Week*, Mar. 28, 1994, pp. 158–163.

Nevis, E. C., DiBella, A. J., and Gould, J. M. "Organizations as Learning Systems." Sloan School of Management Working Paper no. 3567–93. Cambridge, Mass.: MIT Press, 1993.

Nevis, E. C., DiBella, A. J., and Gould, J. M. "Understanding Organizations as Learning Systems." *Sloan Management Review*, 1995, *36*, 73–85.

Nevis, E. C., Lancourt, J., and Vassallo, H. G. *Intentional Revolutions: A Seven-Point Strategy for Transforming Organizations*. San Francisco: Jossey-Bass, 1996.

Nonaka, I. "The Knowledge-Creating Company." *Harvard Business Review,* Nov.-Dec. 1991, pp. 96–104.

Pedler, M., Burgoyne, J., and Boydell, T. *The Learning Company: A Strategy for Sustainable Development.* London: McGraw-Hill, 1991.

Peters, T. *Liberation Management.* New York: Knopf, 1992.

Prahalad, C. K., and Hamel, G. "The Core Competence of the Corporation." *Harvard Business Review,* May-June 1990, pp. 79–91.

Schein, E. *Organizational Culture and Leadership: A Dynamic View.* (2nd ed.) San Francisco: Jossey-Bass, 1992.

Schein, E. "Three Cultures of Management: The Key to Organizational Learning." *Sloan Management Review,* 1996, *38,* 9–20.

Schmidt, W. H., and Finnigan, J. P. *The Race Without a Finish Line: America's Quest for Total Quality.* San Francisco: Jossey-Bass, 1992.

Semler, R. *Maverick.* New York: Warner Books, 1993.

Semler, R. "Why My Former Employees Still Work for Me." *Harvard Business Review,* Jan.-Feb. 1994, pp. 64–74.

Senge, P. M. *The Fifth Discipline: The Art and Practice of the Learning Organization.* New York: Doubleday, 1990.

Senge, P. M., and others. *The Fifth Discipline Handbook: Strategies and Tools for Building a Learning Organization.* New York: Doubleday, 1994.

Shrivastava, P. "A Typology of Organizational Learning Systems." *Journal of Management Studies,* 1983, *20,* 7–28.

Sitkin, S. B. "Learning Through Failure: The Strategy of Small Losses." *Research in Organizational Behavior,* 1992, *14,* 231–266.

Srivastva, S., Cooperrider, D. L., and Associates. *Appreciative Management and Leadership: The Power of Positive Thought and Action in Organizations.* San Francisco: Jossey-Bass, 1990.

Stata, R. "Organizational Learning: The Key to Management Innovation." *Sloan Management Review,* 1989, *30,* 63–74.

Tomassini, M. L. "Apprendimento Organizzativo [Organizational Learning]." *Kybernetes,* 1991, *42,* 18–25.

Torbert, W. R. *Managing the Corporate Dream.* New York: Dow Jones Irwin, 1987.

Torbert, W. R. "Managerial Learning, Organizational Learning: A Potentially Powerful Redundancy." *Journal of Management Learning,* 1994, *1,* 57–70.

Ulrich, D., Jick, T., and Von Gunow, M. A. "High-Impact Learning: Building and Diffusing Learning Capability." *Organizational Dynamics,* 1993, *22,* 52–66.

Watkins, K. E., and Marsick, V. J. *Sculpting the Learning Organization:Lessons in the Art and Science of Systemic Change*. San Francisco: Jossey-Bass, 1993.

Weick, K. "Enacted Sensemaking in Crisis Situations." *Journal of Management Studies*, 1988, *25*, 305–317.

Wenger, E. "Communities of Practice: The Social Fabric of a Learning Organization." *Healthcare Forum Journal*, 1996, *39*(4), 20–26.

Index